Reflections on Waiting for the Mail Train

Ed Mabrey

Copyright ©2018 Ed Mabrey for Grumble Press LLC All rights reserved. Published in the United States of America.

No part of this book may be reproduced or transmitted in any form, or by any means, electronic or mechanical, including photocopying, recording or by any information storage or retrieval system without permission from the publisher.
Layout and design: Ed Mabrey
Cover Art: Ed Mabrey

edmabrey.com
grumblepress.com

CONTENTS

THE CONTAINER TRAIN	1
Around Midnight with Lady Day	2
A Brass Trumpet Stuffed with Dirt	5
A Dog's Life	9
C is for Cookie/ C is for Confrontation/ C is for Choice	14
Bitter	19
Couch	23
Firstborn	31
If You Give a Man a Cookie	35
Letter to Greyjoy and Nipsy Russell	38
Nigger Girl	46
THE INTERURBAN PASSENGER TRAIN	47
Barkbite	48
Child's Play	51
Apnea	56
Kiss Me Kate	59
Dreamweaver	60
Unbroken	62
Oral Prayer #1	65
Life According to Ani	66
The Passion of the Christ	70
SHADOWLANDS #1	74
She Was Section 8/He Her Only Contractor	78
Tarzan Rides the F Train	79
Teddy	81
The Ring	84
God Made Dirt and Dirt Don't Hurt	87
Paul's Purgatory Walk to the Lonesome Valley	89

Juno Se Mama	92
THE MAIL TRAIN	**95**
Séance	96
In The Name of Our Father	101
Heart of Steel	109
Marrow	116
Mother's Milk	117
In the Wake of the Shadow	122
A Pocketknife is not a Plaything: Instructions for my Son	124
Pugilism, Round One: Che Guevara vs. Biggie Smalls	126
Duke the Moon	129
Collette Sims	132
A Hero's Welcome: Richard Pryor on His Way Home from the Motherland	137
For the Easter Yellow Marshmallow Peep, Smashed on the Department Store Floor	141
Jesus and Mary Magdalene- The Last Night Together, the Final Miracle	142
Why They Call Me Tina	144
Blue Baby	149
Rejection Letter	152
Loving Constantine	156
Longina	157
Staccato	159
Straight Edged Razor and the Lustful Wrist	161
Weeds and Roy Ayers	163
Robert Johnson: Live at the Dockery Plantation	166

What follows is my book Waiting For The Mail Train, a collection of poems published and released around 2009-2010. I am typing this in April of 2018. Much has changed since then.

At that time I was madly and deeply in love with someone, I even dedicated some of the poems in this book to her, considered her to be a muse of a certain fashion. No, this isn't the part where I start bashing an ex, I've never trusted anyone who does that (once you've moved out of the phases of breakup/grief/saying things you don't mean) because what does it say about you to say such things about someone you claimed to have loved?

Anywho, I have always been fond of trains, even before I could see the obvious metaphor they represent in human existence. The slow move that becomes a steady and deceiving pace by which your life can go by. The price one pays to travel the paths one chooses. And of course, the people you meet along the way. No matter how horrible or amazing the individuals, two things have always been a certainty in my mind; you start the path alone and you will end it the same way. This isn't depressing, just a sober fact.

I was living in Phoenix, Arizona (my second stint at trying to love someone in that state, the first time was in Tucson). Poetry had been a regular part of my life since around 1998, I had done the open mic thing, some slams, won some major events, toured the country and generally was enjoying life. I had several poetry shows I was running, a small circle of friends and a woman I was prepared to marry.

Now? I don't remember most of the people from that era of my life and rarely speak to the ones that still are within my orbit. That woman I was going to marry got married to someone else and has a great family from what I've heard. I left Phoenix, Arizona after selling most of what I owned and drove what few belongings I kept, to Charlotte, North Carolina.

The train doesn't change, just the car you're in. The car I am currently in has me looking back at the work in this book with equal parts pride and slight embarrassment. Proud of some of the work in here and wondering what happened to the guy who wrote it. Embarrassed at how I can't recall what moved me to write some of the poems, embarrassed at how I can recall what moved me to write some of the poems, neither in a shame-on-me way, more of a muffled chuckle and hand-slap against forehead way.

I am giving you a ticket to the car this book lives in. It is part of the train I don't visit often, I have moved my belongings further up into a car closer to the engine. These days my interest isn't in the viewing car with its all glass everything for maximum 360 degree views. I now yearn to be where the coal gets fed to the fire, to learn how this train moves, see who is driving the damn thing and watch them closely, so that I might one day take those duties over. But for you I leave this book with poems from slams, others that I have never uttered aloud on any stage anywhere. I am certain some things might offend since the allowable words, terms, and views of

2009 are nowhere near the new world we live in now. So if somethings jabs you a little, my apologies, just know like the rest of the world, I have grown much since that time, but if I were to edit this book based on where I am at now with my writing and with a revision/edit eye? I am certain most of these poems would be revised severe enough to not be the same and others wouldn't ever see the light of day. But that is ego and pride, two things I try to keep at bay at least on the page. I believe the vast majority of the poems here have a good shelf life and won't feel dated in any way.

On another note, I am happy to see some of the quotes from peers and friends in this book and think of how far those people have come in their lives. They were doing good work then and each of them have since made names for themselves in their respective fields. For you reading this, I am leaving those quotes and the honors listed along with their authors as is for posterity sake. You might recognize a name or two and think of all they've done and wonder why it isn't listed here. Remember, the train car you're going to be in is circa 2007-2009.

Back then, this book had been dedicated to the woman I was going to marry and to my son. Now? It is dedicated to my son, my mother, her husband, and to you, you reading this with no idea what you've got yourself into. You foolish and beautiful enough to still believe in the written and spoken word in such strange days as the ones we live in now, 2018. And this book is dedicated to those who will never get to move from one train car to the next, forever stuck on the one they were killed on by cowardly bigots. And to the me of that era, the one who took a chance to put this book together in the first place, never knowing where it might go or take us. I am still trying to live up to the memory of my own self. And to Tara Betts, a wonderful writer and educator who didn't hesitate to offer her help and edit this book way back then. Her gentle guidance has been a great teacher over the years.

I am typing this in Philadelphia, PA. Outside my hotel room the wind and rain scream as if they want to join me in this hotel room. Earlier today two Black men were waiting for a friend to meet them at a Starbucks here in Philly. The manager called the police because they were standing in a coffee spot and hadn't bought anything yet. Several officers rushed to the scene and arrested them just as their friend was arriving. I wonder how that will turn out. That is one story on this train. The artist, Prince, died without a will. Lawyers are figuring out his net worth and how to split up what with whom. I wonder who will get the music. I think of how many Black authors of books or songs died penniless or their families starved because they gave up, sold, or lost the rights to their own written creations. That's another reason I am cataloging my time in this train car, to be a resource for others once I am long gone.

The Charlotte, North Carolina train car I have been sitting in for the past 5 plus years no longer suits me. The porter has punched my ticket and informed me I can go into the next car ahead, another step closer to the engine. I wonder what that train car has in store for me, what things I might see, who I'll meet, what stories are there waiting to be written

"Today, on a quiet July Sunday morning when the mail train whistle cries across the valley, one wonders what restless spirits stir in the old churchyard and what they would tell us from their graves about life and forgiveness"
Joe Whitten

"When the first train, the container train, comes through, we know it is time to put the potatoes on the fire. When the next train, the interurban passenger train, comes through, it is time for a break and to cook the chorizo and bacon on the fire and eat them with the potatoes. In the afternoon, very late, the mail train comes past, and it is time to go back. That is the train I am waiting for." Benjamin Romeo- viticulturalist

THE CONTAINER TRAIN

Around Midnight with Lady Day

She sings to forget.
The moment is a window.
She never intended to be
transparent.

Take your time old girl,
the words are there
seated on that couch
you call a tongue,
let 'em find their legs.

Put your hand on that old man's
metal neck, whisper secrets in
his mouth.
Secrets full of earth and thrown gravel
from the ceaseless spin of a tour bus,
secrets rich with sugared words
on fallen angels, and flightless saviors.

Clear, up front,
like the "Whites Only"
sign to your right.
Unnecessary tales
such as the "Coloreds"
sign out of reach on your left.

Secrets that bubble,
overflow off your lips
like a promise,
but don't do that.

Promise.
Keep that word buried
in your handbag,
in your footlocker,
somewhere your soul can't find.

Okay, for just a moment,
remember-before Harlem;
Mobile to Atlanta, Chattanooga
to Memphis, a juke joint in
Charlotte, Louisville,
Lexington, Cincy, Dayton,
Cleveland. Detroit, Chicago,
Chicago, Joliet, Chicago,
Philadelphia, some rib spot on
Broadway, Harlem…

Bury that smile girl,
deep down where they can't see it
and you can't lose it again.
Hide it the same way
long summertime sleeves
protect the world from
your needle-pointed arms,
those tattletale train tracks
that used to be good veins.

Blanket it beneath that warm sheet that
disguises your jones shakes.
Close the doors of your eyes,
mute all passion from your soul.

Almost done.
Take your bow,
encore.
Sloe gin fizz.
Heat that spoon,
put your hand on
that young boy's
hypodermic neck,
let him kiss your arm
in the sweet spot he's carved.

Hear a tour bus rev its engine,
in the rushing flood, a red-faced
monkey dances to your tune.

Keep singing.
After you quit caring,
after you forget
every secret
you meant to hide
you'll still be singing
'bout Harlem.

A Brass Trumpet Stuffed with Dirt
for Steph's Dad

is there any sound like the single trumpet? a
lonely solo in the middle of big bands?
do you sing now Satchmo?
is your voice heard behind the veil?
is your legacy intact beyond the grave?

in the grunts of long days working,
in the sweat from cutting summer lawns,
in the grease which drips onto your oil
laden coveralls in the eyes that say never quit,

in the house you built out of love and caring,
in the laughter of children playing in your yard,
in the smile of a wife dancing to your tune.

your melody is riper for the pain you bear,
your blues in a world gone plastic, sterile, mad.
your fingers never falter when playing chords of loyalty,
fidelity is your score. you mark time under God's eye.

the children, your children march now.
soldiers with their father's names across
their chests. your belt, the measuring rod by
which others are defined.
your love, the barometer for their souls.

mothers serve chicken soup and heal wounds,
mothers give hugs unequaled and show us what
the perfect song can look like, mothers are like the
sun, bright and warm, nourishing and untouchable.

but fathers are mystics, voodoo men,
soldiers who see too much of the world
to not be changed.
fathers are the bluesmen of the earth,
their music rooted in the dirt from which we come,
their melodies dangerously beautiful like nature,
reminding us what is pretty can kill you, if not treated
right, if not appreciated, if not respected.

fathers play songs in tones muddied with their intent: a yell
to get on a porch or sidewalk—a song of safety.
a scream to cut out that racket—a plea for peace.
a holler to not talk back—a lesson in obedience.
a sigh of disapproval—an understanding that
soon he will have to let you go.

most of all, a man gives silence when trying
to accept his fate, when trying to speak with
his God, when letting you learn to make
choices, when fighting back tears so you
might forever think him strong and
invincible.

a big band, full of women play the most beautiful
melodies on the surface of the sun. the one man in the
band sits in the rain on earth playing seemingly
simple notes.
keeping the mundane away from
what he holds spectacular.

playing songs of imperfection, human lowly
songs of the field hand and fisherman, unpretty
tunes of the disciplinarian,
the quiet song of the night watchman and
sentry who keep the boogeyman away.

the father and husband play songs
of the ever faithful hound that you forget was
once a young and spry pup,
your best friend and companion.
once your guardian angel, now just
an old hound that, like the solo
trumpet, you don't notice is gone
till you don't hear his
howling at the moon.

is any sound more wrenching
than the single trumpet?
put your horn down old man,
we will pick up the melody.
you will not be forgotten,
you will be in our every step
upon your earthen back,
you will dance in our tears
and frolic in our laughter,
you will rejoice in our hard days at work and
breathe in our tired return to home.

you will play your song in nightly
dreams of women in your life, you
will peek out at us from eyes of men
you have touched and borne.

rest your lips and wash your hands
in the cool waters of the River Jordan.
tell your tale and swap your lies
with those on the other side of Galilee.
find your rest knowing we will play your song. it is
the song of man that speaks of earth, the song of
man that speaks through us, your moon is howled
upon, your blues ring forever.

A Dog's Life

Old Hank sat at the foot of the bed trying
to look unaffected by the news but the
truth was it was killing him

He'd paced till his legs ached
Try as he might to find the silver laced lining he
could only smell the oncoming rain
just as sure as the number five would make
dishes rattle in the cupboard
the old woman loved but they never
                                  ever
  fell crashing to the ground like Fletch said they would.

'Betcha fifty cents they drop this time ma'
She would smile infectiously and continue stirring the
mystery broth

he had hated for fifty-nine years but grown accustomed to

I'd sit there thinking,
 if she'd taken him up on just half those bets,
 she'd be a rich woman right now

(or at least she could've hidden the tired
old bills from his thirsty hands and he'd
have had to settle for water
or maybe even a
beer but couldn't've got
hooch he'd been drinking with more

regularity
over the past couple of years.)

It hadn't been like this in the beginning.
I can remember old Fletch coming in covered in soot and
ash
like some granite god
snatching up the then shapely young lady
leaving greasy passion stains on her apron and cheeks

A good week's work brought steaks home and
what's a steak without beer to wash it down?
She'd clean the dishes and he'd sit, watching
her
hips
sway to the music from the Wurlitzer
slowly easing behind her. They would
drop
into a groove and dance nuzzled deeply
into one another
from kitchen
to hallway
to bedroom—
hushing the lights as they went

Later that night he'd sit
on the porch,
take a nip from the flask
of bourbon he stashed
looking at me exclaiming
that the world could get no better.

He was right.
It couldn't.

First the war,
stock market crash,
soup lines longer
than your imagination,
and finally the miscarriage.

                      In between them, the bottle
                            flowed over,
          dulling pain at least for a minute or two.

Beers
to wine
to whiskey
to anything he could get. The
soup line in jail is shorter
Who says this wasn't genius in disguise?

All those years in mines and soot didn't get him.
'Canaries'll stop singing before I do', he'd say.
And he was right.
'World'll stop spinning 'fore I do', he'd say.
And he was right.
'Sun'll stop shining 'for I do', he'd say.
'Shut up and save your strength for the love of Mary!' she'd
yell back from the kitchen; no doubt stirring another pot of
who knows what, the ingredients no longer as important as
the pinch of love,
dash of devotion,

and scoop of understanding that
made him not spill a drop in that
    fuzzy
      overgrown
   mustache.

About eight o'clock last night, a
dish finally crashed against the
rickety floor,
but the train doesn't run til eight-fifteen.

About a minute later, Fletch finally won that
bet though I don't think
the money'll make it to the watering hole.

For the first time in fifty-nine years,
plus two years of formal courting,
he didn't eat everything she brought him and even let some

trickle
down
that old stubborn mustache

She didn't bother getting the bowl up but
    sat right
down
    and dabbed at his face with
    the corner of her old ratty apron
    using her tears to get the soup.

About twelve minutes after eight, I
came to the conclusion
that dogs are not color blind— just
lucky to view the world in simpler
ways
                      and headed for the porch.

I spun around my usual three times
plus one extra for Fletch.
World'll stop spinning fore I do.
At exactly eight-fifteen
the number five came roaring by
There sat old Fletch on top, in his Sunday best
'Gotta go now, Hank.'
I know, Fletch.
'Send the old woman my love will ya'?'
Sure will.
'And tell her to keep the fifty cents til she sees me again.' Will
do.
'One last thing, old boy…'
Yeah, Fletch.
'I can't seem to sing no more. Can you…' Say
no more, Fletch. It'd be my pleasure. I stood
my hind legs up on that porch, sucked in all
the air God had to give me and howled at the
moon, that train, world, universe, hell—even
God himself. Canaries'll stop singing fore I
do, Hank. Canaries'll stop singing fore I do.

C is for Cookie/ C is for Confrontation/ C is for Choice

The cookie monster is real
and wearing killer four-inch heels
with a sleek but smart pinstripe power suit.
If Angela Bassett decided to cut her hair short and
become a shrink, this is how she would look I tell
myself.

Now repeat the words-
Fat is not bad.
You cannot live without fat.
You must eat to live.

If comfort food exists, then
my life has been filled
with Lay-Z-Boy recliners
the size of Boeing 747's.

The cookie monster kicks the backs of your legs when
you're in boot camp running miles. When you were born,
he snuck into the nursery and pulled on your toes so you'd
have fallen arches, not bad enough to get out of the Navy
but enough to ensure you did no more than what was
called for.

Fat is not bad.

Nor are Twinkies if you eat only one and only once in a while.
Nor are chickens if one is cooked and consumed by a family
of four.

Nor are cakes if a knife is used to slice it,
but if you remember eating the first slice then wonder
where the rest of the box went?
 If you find a reason to sit on the kitchen floor at 3 in the
morning and eat straight from the rotisserie pan till only
bones and congealed fat remain?
If you don't bother cutting cake but plop down on the couch
with the whole cake, a container of icing and a fork?

Then, no, fat is not bad.
You are.

The cookie monster knows
the chemical composition
of every edible thing
and ties them to every memory.

Your team won the game?
Go eat.
Your first date?
Go eat.
You're visiting your mom?
Go eat.
Anniversary?
Go eat.
Family reunion?
Go eat.

You're out of school.
Those waking years where veils slowly
lifted away from your friends' eyes have
come and gone for you.

By now you have either become-
The fat kid everyone teases/
The fat kid everyone likes/
The fat kid who is so funny/
The fat kid who is so mean to other fat kids/ The fat kid who is so quiet, and unassuming, and gets along well with others, enjoys burying his head in books, and knows all the pretty girls think of him as the little brother they never had, and all the ugly girls call him names, cause, ugly girls got pride not to mention their own problems.

So you're sitting in the movie theater watching "Chicago" with some girl who looks great but whose name escapes you, and it hits you-
You are cellophane.
Mr. Cellophane, Mr. Cellophane
Won't you say my name?
Mr. Cellophane
You can look right at me
Walk right by me
And never know I'm there
Mr. Cellophane[1]
The problem is not that you're fat.
Have a cookie.
The problem is that you're
you and you're fat.
Have a cookie.

———————————————

Your esteem issues are buried beneath the
mammoth girth you carry.
Have a cookie
Your esteem issues are buried because you
don't trust anyone to care.
Have a cookie.
Your relationships falter because you spend too
much time eating instead of quality time.
Have a cookie.
Your relationships falter because the cute ones have
nothing to say or are blander than the fucking tofu they eat
so you feed them to shut them up and yourself to have
something to do to kill time between now and the next
time you'll sleep together.
Have a cookie.
You can't forge working loving moments
with an average girl because you feel as if
you're looking in a mirror.
Have a cookie.

Things go sour with plain looking or big girls
because they make the mistake of looking up
to you and how low must they be to look up to you?

What happens when they get their shit together
and realize you're not the man they thought you were?
Not as handsome as you appeared in a half empty plate?
Not as debonair when you're not feeding
them chocolates by candlelight?

Not so sexy when she wants to spoon cuz
your stomach gets in the way. What
happens when she discovers that you are
just a man? You will work on the cure
for cancer and a world peace plan as
soon as you figure out how to be seen
for who you are.

Because most days,
you're value meals away
from joyous elation or
a nervous breakdown.
You're Mr. Cellophane.

The only way to kill
the cookie monster
is to snake yourself
around his throat
then shove your skeleton
down his gullet.
Then say fat is not bad,
you must eat to live.

[1]Italicized excerpt consists of lyrics written by John Kander and
Fred Ebb from "Mr. Cellophane" in the musical "Chicago".

Bitter

Not as smooth as a kiss,
more like a trick knee
or an amputated leg
on some homeless cat
that makes your shin itch
when you try not to make
eye contact and pass him by.

Not as warm as a hug,
more like an eight-year-old's loose tooth that
comes out during a bite of tuna melt
at an IHOP, back when they still had funny roofs, or
the nosebleed you got from your best friend in the fifth
grade. You don't mind much except for the mess and
how you'll have to explain that mess later.

Not as intimate as making love,
more like really needing CPR and
getting it from a serpent that
smokes GPC's and starts every
morning with a double espresso.

It leaves you alive,
but the air you've taken in will
more than gag your senses,
it will funk up your very soul.

This is not a bitter poem.

In the beginning you believe,
much like the title of your work that the
sun will come out tomorrow,
every cloud has a silver lining,
the grass is always greener,
and clichés need hugs sometimes too.

In the middle you believe
your work is not that good,
the moon must be working overtime,
or the sun has taken a deserved, overdue vacation,
every cloud proves there are a million shades of gray and
cliché's don't get laid much due to limited conversation.

This is not a bitter poem.

In the end you believe
that all your work is crap,
the sun got arrested for indecent
exposure and clocks are now set by eclipse.
Clouds drip acid that flows up from your eyes and the
next person who quotes something trite will get
strung up by their toes like the person who invented
the term clichés should be.

Because you are not poetic, romantic, suave
Your words nor your presence change lives,
make people reconsider religious choices, and
your voice, no matter how deep, provides you no
depth.

You are broken promises,
unfinished kisses, cold sheets
and warmed leftovers.

You are six numbers dialed
then hang up, emails began
then deleted, letters written
that the wastebasket reads
then speaks to you during
your rousing marathon
nights of internet solitaire, saying-
Hey buddy, quit filling me
with your baggage and using me
for three-pointer buzzer beaters!
Stop shoving notes to the bottom
just to weasel them out later,
make up your mind!

This is now a bitter poem.

You have written Ford and told them
they are building entirely too many
fucking Escorts. By your last count,
there has to be 3,267,429, give or take
a few in your neighborhood alone,
and that was yesterday's numbers.

You're trying to remember the correct number for
the sexy girl you met while wondering if it's too
late, hell, it's only been a couple years maybe she's
been busy.

You can say you've been getting debriefed
because you're in the CIA and well,
you dream imaginary lives often these days
and talk to yourself more but it's okay.

You haven't told anybody
you keep finding her hairs and spend
Sundays looking for hidden cameras,
thinking maybe you're on some reality
show called 'loser'.
Your mom would return your calls more often but
she's tired of debating the fact that you think of
Sade and Phyllis Hyman as up tempo.

In the beginning it was a smooth as a kiss,
in the middle it was as warm as a hug,
in the end it was as intimate as making love.

It is called breaking up.
It is called growing up.
It is called letting go.

This is not a bitter poem.
It's a wake up call.

Couch

1.
In the end there is this,
her embrace is not as warm as it once was but
your hand can trace the grooves that her body
sinking into the couch over the past 30 years
has made.

You two have been sitting on the
same couch for 30 years. That
would not be love, that would be
slightly nasty since Febreze was
only made for mass use about 5
years ago.

It says that for 30 years,
two people have fought, shared, and cared
dared to love and laugh in destiny's face and
begun each day or ended each eve on a couch
in that same house.

2.
The first one wasn't much to speak of.
You both were out of college and money
was tighter than the springs in that
old plaid thing.

Every Saturday night, you two played the
magic hand poker game. One of you, the
braver, or the loser of the coin toss

would stick their hand into the
deep recesses of that tattered
thing until you felt something,
then with teeth gritted, pull
out- Oh my God what is that?
And laugh.

You would try to get up and run, get to
the sink and wash this moldy ace of
spades from your fingertips but he
would hold you still, till his own hand
came from beneath those ancient fibers,
his palm turning upwards to reveal
its unidentifiable royal flush that
smelled slightly of decaying ramen
noodles.

You played this game for three years, never
once bringing up an empty hand and it
always ended the same, no matter who the
winner or loser, the two of you-

washing hands together in the bathroom sink. The
lather the only thing between the two of you, steam
kissing the walls and windows, her leaving scratch
marks of moisture down the back of the glass shower
door, your hips wet and heavy with intent, your
motions so intertwined that the water would become
confused about which one it was running over.

3.
The next couch was from a well bred family,
Scottish tweed flecked with marigold you could see
if your imagination was dotted with sunshine,
for a time it was.

This one wouldn't get past seven months.
It was there on those trustworthy cushions
you two heaved and moaned as one.
The marigolds on the armrests lifted their
imaginary little leaves and outstretched
their petals to catch the falling wine
glass, tipping enough to not stain the
tasseled coverlet.

It was on that same couch that the pregnancy test fell. How
it tumbled and bounced onto the floor below, the plus sign
flipping over like a holy cross rolling down a hill in
Bethlehem.

On that same couch, you were sitting when
the phone rang. You assumed she had went
shopping with your mother. That must be
true, otherwise you never would have
answered the call with so much joy and
hope in your blind voice. The couch was
concrete that day. The arms could not catch
the receiver slipping from your grasp, they
were too busy trying to hold you,

keep you warm. The doctor screamed
from the floor in a distant voice, he
might as well have been on the
moon with a soup can and some
string.

You tried to get up.
Knew the right thing to do would
be to rush to the hospital right now
right now right now get up but you
couldn't.

You had to rest your head on the arm of the couch.
Bury your fears deep in its large shoulders.
Pull your trembling knees up to your chin and cry
tears of what if's and could have beens into its stoic
fabric.

After that, neither of you sat on that couch. For
your anniversary you agreed to buy his and her
recliner chairs, ottomans and matching lamps
that would face each other instead
of being side by side. Not long after that
you could not recall the last time you held hands or
kissed and love making began to be a chore.

4.
You had just been laid off.
She was in night school working towards something that
could get her out of the house more often. The trash can
would jingle on its way to the curb,

full of empty beer bottles and other stronger brews, their
spirits rising upwards mixing the remains of their vapor
with the outside air.

You both were drunk and in the wrong.
Neither of you can recall what was said
but both of you know someone went too far.
There is a plate in pieces on the kitchen tile,
food from the dining room table is scattered down the hall.
One of the chairs smells like Jack Daniel's, her
handprint is fresh on his face, her nightgown is
torn in two. Someone has said *Get your hands
off me,* someone else, *Don't you walk away
when I am talking to you.*

You opened your eyes and found yourself slightly
hung over but sitting on the coffee table staring at
that couch.
The fabric seemed to dance in your inebriated state. You
could see little feet running through fields, on the middle
cushion, disconnected hands were guiding a laughing
voice down a driveway, the training wheels sitting to the
side this time and catching a full dose of the summer
rays. Picnics and birthday parties, skinned knees and
bloodied lips, the pitter patter of feet tipping into the
living room where the Christmas tree stood guard over
the goodies.

To this day you don't recall how the axe got in your hand
but when you raised it over your head and it came down,
a mighty thump cascading through the dimly lit room,
a sound that only steel can make when taken to wood,
it felt right and you swung, and you swung.
You would lift then you would drop.
The axe would thud. The couch began to
creak and cry thud wheeze and moan
thud.

You don't recall when she came in the room but
you could see the hammer in her hand. It still had
the tag dangling on it.
It was to be used to build the bassinet.
Thud.
that you never got to build.
Swing.
and this was where it started.
Thump.
and this is where it should end.
Swing.
That night there was a full moon
though neither of you took the time to notice. Both
of you stood on either side of that couch gnashing
your teeth, arms burning with the fire of the tired
but never stopping, like chain gang workers laying
tracks by the River Styx, your song was each name
you never got to argue over.

He could have been Samuel
She could have been Mary
David
Antoinette
Kyle
Moses
Pearl
Ebony
Lila
Thomas

Between the screams and tears,
the wood chips jumped and flipped out of harm's way. Two
hearts splintered began to fuse together, as hearts can.
When the chest heaving stopped, shoulders slumped and
breaths came in short harsh tears,
the two of you walked through the remains of the
couch into the night and walked into the
bathroom,

washing your hands and picking splinters
from each other's fingers,
easing into the shower to wash and
never was a word spoken. You
started to touch then feel then
remember a tiny kiss given under
the shower's spray so faint that it
might be a memory of better times,
two people so close that the water
became confused which set of lips it
had started on and accidentally wound up
wetting the others.

You did not make love that night
but you consummated reconciliation.
Sex was involved, but is it just sex
when love fills your heart to the point of hurting?
Is it just a couch, a mere piece of furniture,
a creature comfort, when it holds two people so close?

5.
You did not go couch shopping immediately.
There was an agreement that the purchase would be organic,
when the time was right the two of you would just know it.
Couch shopping should not be taken lightly.

The young and foolish
will purchase with only their heart,
the old and bitter only with their
pocket or fears and sensibilities in
tow.
Either way you end up with something that
looks bad but feels nice, or something that
looks great but feels like sitting on a bench
in Central Park, calm yet unnerving. You
should not be able to settle into the couch
immediately, it should show promise that
one day there will be a spot that can recall
your name, that has recorded the memory
of your presence for safe keeping.
This is not felt in a price tag or listed
on the materials tag. This is something
done with the person you will share it with.
This is for the doing.

Firstborn

I remember the dance
The embrace still calls my shadow home
It rests in the maple of our friendship
The serenity only unmasked in our farewells

I am not yet ready for my hand to fall back to my waist
The fingers have ignored your crying eyes
Winds won't threaten this final song
To you, I bid no regrets of yearning

The candles won't burn; the wax stands still
Autumn refuses to give up its chair
Though winter has entered the room
The leaves keep their chlorophyll
My arms branch out, trying to hold you even now
As the teddy bears bid their adieus

Hookers on Main Street attempt to return money made
Their fishnet stockings ensnaring lines of redemption
On Cleveland Avenue a preacher tosses his Lexus car
keys to the bum at the UDF and cries himself home

But again I say no

No to long legs that linger in the edges of my peripheral
No to morning berry juice that begs me drink and forget
No to alley cats mewing for milk which never comes
No to the noose which holds my grandfather's neck

The space heater clicks on even in your absence
There's no plastic on the old windows

It squats like an old sumo wrestler
Determined to warm me through sheer will

I wish to be that space heater
Plug me into the current of this world
And I will speak of your eyes on the lower frequencies
Just beneath your scalp I will live and tickle your dreams

I will warm you with all I have
Even if I am stripped down to mere words
Sew these pages into a cloak and let the shawl
Of my passion keep frost from your soul
If words are all I have then I will erase goodbyes
Stop this poem in midsentence so if it never ends
Then neither can you

If only you'd been born dead in the womb
Suffering would never have had a name
If only dilation was a myth
A hymen, some random thought
But no, cold stainless steel has no
room for probabilities, only truth

In truth, you were born, for a moment
A shooting star in a world of fleas
You took a breath, wrapped your hand around my finger
And left without giving me the chance to say goodbye

I will not rust the water behind my eyes
My vision cannot be clouded with time
Still now my hand remains ever vigilant
If it does not falter then goodbyes cannot begin

So hello my miscarried misammee
My unfinished aspiration
I will tug at this umbilical cord of war till God
removes goodbyes from creation

"When I first met Ed Mabrey he was brooding about something. I offered him a hug and asked if he was okay. He said he was just thinking. The second time I met Ed Mabrey, he was brooding again. Something about consuming the world but being out of mayonnaise. The third time I met Ed Mabrey, he was still at it. Brooding. But there was a smile involved that time. And that laugh making its way up his baritone. This time, he admitted, there was a poem involved."

Dasha Kelly
HBO Def Poet, Founder – StillWater Collective

If You Give a Man a Cookie

The pattern is simple
In the way cigarettes are brilliant
Or guns are brilliant
Or McDonald's chains are brilliant

First it's
Oh how cute
What chubby little legs
What pudgy little cheeks
He's adorable
Have a cookie

Second, you're
shopping at Kmart,
Sears, and Value City
In the husky section
Color choices? Two:
Brown and…brown

Someone says
What a gentlemanly young man
How old is he? Oh. Well, it's just
Baby fat, it'll fade

You look at your mom for understanding,
seconding it'll fade away motion She says
Have a cookie

Third, by the age of fifteen, you've built calluses

All those-
You so fat your stomach got its own zip code
You so fat your designer jeans say to be continued
You so fat you go bra shopping with your grandma

Ragu blood lard ass weeble wobble earthquake
beached whale blubber butt bookman look alike-
Comments slowly trickle salt stained trails down your
steel feathered back

Somewhere along the way cool points are racked up as
you begin to travel in varsity football circles till marching
band girls are overheard saying-He's cute but…fat

The car runs great-just looks like shit
You've got personality
The house is run down but the plumbing is new
You've got character
The soup looks nasty but boy is it good
You've got a sense of humor

You are fat
Overweight obese
large and in charge
Of everything except
Your wilted willpower

First rule of fat club is to tell no one you're in fat club
Denial
Second rule of fat club is to act as if there is no fat club More
denial

Third rule of fat club is if this is your first night at fat club
You've got to eat

And you do
Birthdays holidays weekdays
Have a cookie
Breakfast lunch dinner
Have a cookie
In between meal meals
Fast food fancy food
Happy? Eat Sad? Eat Mad? Eat
Game on? Eat commercial? Eat
Lady loves you? Eat Lady left you? Eat
Twelve course meals at Ryan's Gotta
loosen your pants to breathe
Too tired to even tie your shoe but before we go home
I need to stop and get some milk
And what's milk without a cookie?

And if you give a fat
Yes I am fat
Man
A cookie
His hand will cheer
His stomach will scream
Yes
But his eyes will ask
Why?

Letter to Greyjoy and Nipsy Russell

(for Mike McGee)
Nipsy Russell passed away October 2, 2005

This was written by blogger Greyjoy, Orlando, FL, October 18, 2004:

For the past two weeks, I've had this compulsion. It's taken me some time to even realize that it's a pattern. Even without being aware of it when my mind wanders, I repeat this name over and over again in my head—Nipsy Russell, Nipsy Russell, Nipsy Russell, Nipsy Russell—until I suddenly realize that I'm doing it, and I think (or blurt aloud), "Who is Nipsy Russell?"

I feel like he (or she?) was an actor on an old sitcom from the 70s. Like "Good Times" or "The Jeffersons" or "What's Happenin'" or something.

I have no idea how Nipsy Russell slipped into my lexicon. All I know is repeating the name over and over has a soothing effect. Try it. There's something about the name that just rolls off the tongue (or the mind). It's like sticking a key in a lock and feeling all the teeth give in. Nipsy Russell. Ah, like the Balm of Gilead. Like a cool rag on a hot brow. Like mother's milk. Like lollipops and ice cream with rainbow sprinkles.

Maybe it doesn't matter who Nipsy Russell is (or was). The bastard could be dead for all I know. Maybe it just matters what Nipsy Russell means to me. Not just some compulsively repeated name, but a key into some back door in my gray matter.

Nipsy,

You being considered
the poet laureate of television,
I feel I can speak to you, one man
to another, one poet to another fellow.
I will not sugarcoat this.
There is no time for it and
to be blunt,
no need.

You will be forgotten soon and
soon enough your name will be
a joke. Your memory, just so
much fodder for a screenwriter,
inspiration for a hack.

Don Cheadle will collect your Oscar.
Wynton Marsalis and Quincy Jones will
hold the olive branch long enough to
compose a proper score.
50 Cent and Talib Kweli
will split video time
with Usher and Beyonce.
Someone will dance.
Someone will sing.
Everyone will buy in,
but no one, no one
will remember you.

Nipsy, the militant.
God made your skin
darkest to hide your fear
and trembling lips.
Your teeth so white
to infuse those who
would hate you with
warmth undeniable.

You sang and danced.
They called you fool,
Tom, and servant.
But they didn't see you.
Those bleached white choppers, a
perfect picket fence grin, didn't
hear the hinges grinding against
each other.
The steady steam whistle
of your warning,
"Hurry up!"
"Go now while I got 'em distracted!"

We never listened.
Didn't hear the Huey P. Newton in
your $20,000 Pyramid jokes.
Ignored the Malcolms, both Little
and X, when Dean Martin
would call you boy
and say, "See you later, Nipsy."
All the while his eyes screaming, "Nigger!"

And you'd say, "Not if I see you first." Your
eyes, those basset hound implants never
leaving his but looking past him, past the
cirrhosis and fake backdrop.
A glare traveling over power lines
right into our homes,
leaping from our TV screens,
waiting till that moment of moments
between show and commercial, that
twilight of a nanosecond and whispered
to us,
"Keep your chin up,
but more important,
keep your eyes open."

We will soon forget,
some of us already have,
how you pulled such high marks at
the University of Cincinnati. How the
most bigoted students in one of the
most racist of towns could never
bring himself to hit this impossibly
dark man.
Was it the smile Nipsy?
The constant sorrow eyes?
Or the skin that hung on your face like
so much dark matter? A black hole
threatened,
"If you hit me, you might not get
your hand back. Might not ever see it again."

Right now, someone doesn't
know your Broadway walk.
Never saw you take the stage.
The other actors, no matter how
hard they tried,
could never hold their face still.
Could never stay in character.
Would look up, flinch, or blink
when it was your entrance cue. A
universe collapsed in on itself the
day you were born, it fell into your
face.

How many of your own people
have called you sellout?
A poor man's Sammy Davis. No
Rat Pack to call your own. You
could not afford them
nor did you desire their company, or
their chattering concubines. The
whites looking at you in awe of what
God can do when
he feels like creating art called man.
The blacks skittish, and afraid.
Too much history in your wrinkle free skin, too
much beauty in a face
that bridges old worlds and new.

You were no sellout.
You stood between a Diana Ross, and
a Michael Jackson. You stood
between
a little girl lost and looking for a father, and
a boy trying to run from his. You stood
between Dorothy and Scarecrow.
The fear and the flesh.
You were a tin man,
beat up, dented,
but never down.
Made up of different discarded scraps,
resourceful.
You wept when your journey seemed too
much to bear,
and in doing so let a little boy know it
was ok to cry sometimes just as long as
you didn't quit.
You danced and sang when jubilant,
and reminded a child that gay means happy.
You hid your blackness beneath a thin, metal layer, saying,
"You are human first, a man second, and black last."
When I thought all your lessons were taught,
and returned to ditties, jingles, and flying monkeys, you
swayed to the left, to the right.
If a man is not willing to bend a little, he
will break.

You stood between two superstars at their peaks
and dwarfed them, sucked them in at a perilous, breakneck
speed. See underneath all that gun metal grey makeup. Beneath
the clanking parts and clanging gears.
The one thing that never needed oil, your smile,
white supernova fighting for space in
your dark matter face. As I write this,
someone is melting you down,
recycling your good parts,
scrapping the rest. But the smile?
That we will never forget.
When all else is gone,
we will remember
your smile, and the secret
lessons held inside.

From Greyjoy's blog October 18, 2004
*Maybe it doesn't matter who Nipsy Russell is (or was, the
bastard could be dead for all I know), maybe it just matters
what Nipsy Russell means to me. Not just some compulsively
repeated name, a key into some back door in my gray matter.
It has the same effect on me that The Litany Against Fear has
on*
Paul Atreides in "Dune":

I shall not Fear
Fear is the mind killer
I shall not Fear
Fear is the little death that brings on total
oblivion I shall face my fear

I shall allow it to pass over me and through me
Then I shall look with the inner eye
Where the Fear has gone there will be nothing
Only I shall remain.[2]
Or in my case:

Nipsy Russell Nipsy Russell Nipsy Russell
Nipsy Russell
Nipsy Russell Nipsy Russell

---

2 The lines of this stanza are a chant of Bene Gesserit in Frank Herbert's science fiction work *Dune*. The Bene Gesserit comprise exclusive sisterhood and force in this universe and they recite this in dangerous times to focus and calm themselves. The beginning and ending of this piece are excerpts from ka-tet.blogspot.com.

Nigger Girl

She is black tissue paper
constantly crushed, folded,
tucked in corners, manipulated,
pushed in the hollows of bags,
left forgotten in boxes.

She is measured, judged, compared to
others for the proper size, the correct
amount of blackness, as if to say one
could have too much or too little.
She is aborted and
continuously conceived.

Her edges are frayed, cut to fit,
often torn for effect.
Her voice, a crumbled rustling of dead
leaves, uprooted from their tree, without
the strength to find home.

She is the ultimate trophy, sought out, hunted,
cornered, purchased, bought, sold, then
brought home, shoved into some
uncomfortable form or shape.
Without consent, she is used to wrap
and protect, and show off finite gifts
which we treasure most.

We leave her for dead in some forgotten place
in our home 'til the need to smooth out her
wrinkles best we can, and use her,
comes once again.

THE INTERURBAN PASSENGER TRAIN

Barkbite

Behind her wooden door
eye sap runs like pain.
Behind the bark of her lids
syrup starts to flow.

In the other room,
maybe the kitchen,
more than likely the garage,
he sits in that old Buick,
the one he never gets around
to fixing and looks at his fist
and wonders where the splinters came from.

Upstairs a teddy bear begs
for someone to sew him a mouth.
Somewhere in that room, probably in
the bed,
a girl counts stars behind her eyes
and waits for the boogeyman.

In the hallway, ten paces from her door
a bottle falls from daddy's hand,
empty, its mouth open but nothing
to say. His hand trembles, grabs the
doorknob.

In the dining room, a boy stands between
mom and dad trying to use his fledgling branches

to deflect his father's swipes on mother. Blood
on his young leaves, when he looks into his
father's eyes, sees his reflection and becomes a
man.

In a room with one chair,
a poet writes words he does not know
as fact by sight but feels the names of
each person as they jump onto the
page.

It is his job, not to bask in the melancholy, not to
tell tales for the sake of plumbing depths of the
human stain, not to pull fools' tears nor grant the
ignorant access to heaven, not to impress nor
depress, not to suffer unto little children, nor
redeem himself.

He does because he has yet to get the
tellings and engagements right and he
fears each time he falters another
blow is delivered because he didn't
listen, he didn't write it right.

But it's not your pain, so why care?
Tell me, you ever see the fading remnants of a
woman's black eye stare out at you
as if it were the eye of your woman or mother?
Have you passed a child in the store,
whose mouth was drawn tight but his eyes
begged for someone to kidnap him?

Take him anywhere but where he was? Have you ever
watched a girl pray for death because life became too
much for a seven-year-old?

I didn't think so.
I will speak for those who have no voice till
mine gives out and theirs grow strong.

I heard a poem once about a happy family, a
place with no pain where everyone got along,
where the night held no screams and daytime
trees had fruit and sun in their stride, where
laughter was the only communicable disease
and everyone was infected.
A place where poems like this
remained unwritten.
I heard a poem once about a happy family.
It was the best fiction I've ever heard.

Child's Play

You asked what I'd like to do tonight
You asked what I'd like to do tonight and I just stared at you
You asked what I'd like to do tonight so told you

let's fill up the tank and drive till it runs out
go to sleep in the car
fill it up in the morning
and drive back home

let's trade lunches
swap football pencils
gimme some of your grape Now and Laters and I'll
let you have some of my Lemonheads

kiss me on the cheek with daffodils
till my smiles are stained sunshine yellow write my
name plus yours on your book cover
or help me make my paper footballs for fifth period or
help me get quarters into my penny loafers and you can
have any Blowpop you want even sour apple
THAT'S love

Let's go to school and play
hopscotch four-square tetherball
I don't give a damn what the kids say

Let's take our dress shoes off and play basketball
in our church clothes with an old milk crate and a tennis ball

then go behind Ms. Harmon's class and neck now
that we think we know how to do it right

Let's play Superfriends
I'll be Aquaman, Batman, Robin, Superman, Green
Lantern, Black Lightning, Green Arrow, the Wonder
Twins and their little monkey Gleek You be
WonderWoman
and not cause I'm greedy but in
my state of regression I can admit
that you've always been more
than I can handle so it comes out
even

Let's play house
I'll come in from work tired and you won't have anything
worthwhile to eat except for some goddamn mud pies and
make believe tea and you'll nag about how our Holly
Hobbie
doll baby children have kept you running all day and the
Slinky
dog pissed on the new couch and the Easy Bake Oven is on the
fritz again when am I going to get a real job so we can get a
new
Green Machine the Big Wheel's got a rock in one of the tires
and
the alignment's screwed and why can't we be more like
Barbie

and Ken, he has a job at Tonka and they have a Corvette and they
have a vacation house in Malibu and they have house parties and
don't give you that 'it's cause he's white and from the burbs and
the man is trying to keep you down shit' and Raggedy Ann called
saying Raggedy Andy's been drinking too much, maybe I should
take him out and try to find out what's wrong and the plaster is falling
from the Tinker Toy roof when am I going to get around to fixing it and…

On second thought, let's play hide'n'seek
Let's watch Willy Wonka while eating
all the Hershey bars we want till we get shakes

Let's eat Pop Rocks and chase them
down with Pixie Sticks poured
in Pepsi then stare at the clouds and acid trip Let's
see who can hold their breath the longest

Let's see who can survive on just one man
on Ms. Pac-Man the longest or Defender or
Burgertime or Gorf or Asteroids or Donkey
Kong or Tron or Mario Bros.

Let's play checkers
Let's jump rope

Let's play marbles, jacks, go fish,
old maid, tonk, I declare war Let's
sneak into a movie
Let's tease Mr. Vandyke's dog Let's
see who can skip the longest jump the
highest
run for no other reason than to
try and leave time behind

Let's play Star Wars in old Halloween masks
Watch Captain Kangaroo Electric Company Bugs
Bunny Plastic Man Battlestar Gallatica Buck
Rogers Captain Caveman Johnny Quest

Play Ring Around the Rosie
London bridge's Tag
Red light-Green light
Duck Duck Goose
Musical Chairs

I can't promise all the time to be a gentleman
Sometimes I might bump you out your seat This
way I can help you up and be the hero and other
times I might flop on the floor so I can look up to
you do you know I've always looked up to you?

Let's carve our names on a tree
if I can steal a knife out the kitchen
without getting caught but you're
worth the risk
my name next to yours is

worth the butt whipping

Let's stay out after the streetlights come on
Your smile by moonlight is worth a week's punishment and I'll
run home, my feet not even touching the ground

I'll look at my mom and say
Mother, you may chain my body to these four walls You
can pull a switch from yonder field and strike me till thy
arms wither and die
Confine me to my humble room for 1,000 years but
my heart rides free tonight
She'll say Get your little ass in that room and quit
sipping out of Anthony's momma's cup when she
ain't looking

Let's forget books and big words
plays concerts special events nice
clothes and manicures balances and
atm withdrawals pms and sixty-hour
work weeks cell phones computers

You asked me what I'd like to do tonight and I stared at you
You asked me what I'd like to do tonight and I told you I'm
doing it

Apnea

I am constantly haunted by
storms and metal things, sharp
edges and temptation, ripped
flesh and gouged eyes, all
things reflected or felt.

Ghosts sit for me
in empty file cabinets and untended calendars on
piles of letters and yellowed pages,
in used bed sheets and tear-soaked pillows, in
muted phones and powerless plastic and bus
schedules and identification and pocket change
and weights and dust and mold and mops and
shovels,
in plastic windows and electrician's tape, in
to-do lists and phone books, in remote
controls and slipcovers.

They belch their disgust
when I sit on their images.
They expel Black Death
in my calloused feet
and sore teeth and memos and messages
and lost numbers, forgotten friends and
light bulb's sting.

They call for my flesh when
darkness carves itself upon
entombed automobiles and flat tires,
while flashlights seek purchase in
jaundiced stares,

They bite my thighs,
the punctures feel
like old girlfriends
and raped fences,
untilled earth
and burnt cotton.

They kiss me
and it tastes like
Dragons' spittle
and beetle dung
and mourners' bread
and Spanish lipstick
and cancerous breezes
on Dead Seas
or gap-toothed smiles
on rotted corpses.

They hold me still
like chain-linked piranhas or
barking Chihuahuas, the in-
laws' embrace, the kiss of
electric chairs and the secrets
nooses know.

They hold me for judgment
guillotine, trial, weeping song
and dance, brine, lightning and
cities.

They relieve themselves
in my hollow corners.

Their urine reeks
of overripe cotton candy,
brimstone, red fingernails, wax,
black eyes, and warnings.

They haunt me daily
and sit by my bedside
when I am sick or sleeping.

Shiny finger of a knife
under my nostrils
looking for signs of hope,
checking for glimmers
of shallow fog,
terminal dew,
quiet surrender.

Kiss Me Kate

never be afraid to take a step closer to me
believe each movement of your feet is a
song gaining its voice
and my loving you is a privilege not a choice of
course I fail in your eyes
it was what I was made to do but
I'll never stop my flying
towards your smile
let the wax melt from my wings I'll
make candles that only sing when lit
by the fire in your heart
I stole the laughter from a school-
room full of children and placed
them beneath my ribs so when you tickle me
the piano of my body will play keys of all our kids can I
be your only regret and you my one good deed I'll be
Isaac to your Icarus
the only thing we'll need is our hands to
build a tomorrow better than our now
I don't say I love you cause love can't
handle the burden
I'm certain on God's dresser is a picture of
 you for inspiration
when she has writer's block and her lover
hasn't called in six days
how many ways do I love you
one for every breath one for every step
more than hookers love promises and winos need sunrise step
into my arms and never be cold kiss me quick and we'll never
grow old, kiss me quick and we'll never grow old, make me
young again

Dreamweaver

I've learned the difference between
being a man and a boy,
is a boy wipes the tears from his eyes, the
man lets them fall.
The boy storms out the room screaming fuck you and
the man wonders if you'll ever call.
The boy wants to fuck or make love cause to him it's the
same,
the man just wants to sleep by your side
and knows in that there is no shame.
the boy demands,
the man hopes.
the boy gives up,
the man copes.
The man falls in love each time you kiss,
the boy protects his heart so the point gets missed.

Please don't let this be our goodbye,
keep the dogs in the closet at bay.
I don't always say the right thing but at least I
got something to say, when it all ends and the
dreamweaver rises from her loom

I want to look around the room and see
the quilts of love we made and the
shade that graces your face from the
tree we planted together protecting us
like a smile through all this stormy
weather-or not we make it to old age
let's at least make it together,
this life is just an old stage
where actors must die for the story to get better.

So let me tell it now tell it here tell it loud, of
the days when we were young,
I was a gun and you a nurse
bent on trying to heal my trigger temper
and pull the gunpowder from my cheeks.
I was a wayfarer bold with a heart too cold
to give you what you seek, I tinged your snow grey
and bade you stay for just another season.
What could it hurt to accuse each other of treason
beneath bed sheets made of laughter?
Till you added an s to my laughter
and made it slaughter every son and daughter we
never got the chance to spawn.

It's taken years but I know life must go on-this
winding road, like others, lead to the carnival, my
ticket in hand. My cage awaits,
I am the first act in a three-ring circus.
The curtains part-ladies and gentlemen,
I present the man who lives without a heart. The
difference between being a boy and a man is a boy
wipes his tears
and the man lets them fall down his face
to that dark part, that blank spot, that old spark, his
empty heart.

Unbroken
For A.G.

There's a woman sitting in the tree
Her kisses are made of maple
I ask for her lips
She accepts no part of me
But my ears
Her branches
Tender poplar
They scratch my soft parts
Write the word 'soul' in Sanskrit
In her own flesh
She rips leaves away as discarded fingertips
Places them in her mouth and chews
Removes the pulp
And places it over my heart
Like a salve
God has stripped her bare
Made her a star of old films
Where she stood with her sisters
While humans dropped bombs
To test their mettle
Watched, as her kin were blown into shrapnel
She is white as bleached bones
Perfect without her bark
I wish to climb her branches
All her limbs are curved, petrified towards the east
I awaken to the smell of burning pine in my nose
And fresh pages, blank, in an unbound book
Save one inscription
You are no good to me dead
You must live to tell our story

Write on my body
And make me whole again
Forever yours
The unbroken bough
Your tree nymph

"When I first met Ed Mabrey, he was pretending an erotic poem for the Nationals 2006. The women swooned at first, his baritone obviously too intense for their faint hearts. And the fellas nodded in a respectful manner, if they too were blessed with the tone of Mr. Mabrey, they too would play coy at an erotic poetry reading. But Ed is more than voice. He is breath and song and marrow and fire. His words are alive and if given the chance, they will swell your insides with hope."

Mahogany L. Browne
Slammistress of Nuyorican Poets Cafe, Owner of PoetCD.Com, Publisher Penmanship Books, Writer, Facilitator & Mom

Oral Prayer #1

If I could have one wish
it would be to grow gills
and be down on you
like this, forever swimming
in your waters, your taste,
an ever present thing.
Ease through my mouth-
breathing you to live.

Life According to Ani
(for Andrea Gibson)

There were no stars in the sky that night
No rain or unicorns to blame
In fact, aside from the fairies in your eyes
Holding those rubies in their palms
There was no one around at all

I kept the horses just like I promised
Kept the promise like I wanted to keep you-
Tight and warm against my chest
Full and spirited
Like a sprite high on her own dust
You laughed
That laugh that made me snort dandelions out my nose
You chuckle so hard you spit your heart out
And we laugh as the dog drags it all around the house

Out into the yard we gave chase
I was a tired sorcerer with a carpet for a ride
And you, a wayward drifter with a smile made of doves
And a tongue made from butterfly wings

Do you remember that night
We flew past Jericho mile
Bartered with the gypsies for
their magic lamps
Rubbed every one till we found one with a genie
You tucked him behind you ear like a story
And we headed for all points south and west

You kissed me and took the learning from my mind

Left me that way, scant inches from a cloud getting in my hair
I know you think I was sad or embarrassed from your
forward ways
I didn't speak so I could keep those wings in my mouth
Chewed those fluttering monarchs till their crowns slid down
my throat
Each rib laughed and welcomed your presence Like
the shadows welcome sun on concrete
Or trees giggle with the incessant chatter of birds

Those ears of yours, precious bell towers
To hear how my name sounds inside your head
This I yearn to know
Let others wage war
I will kneel in your gardens
Plant flowers in your image
Build a shrine on your rounded belly
Pray to God until he teaches me
To say your name as He intended

My glistening piñata
Is there any taste not manifested by your lips Any
tide not dictated by your hips
Any ship's captain that doesn't set his compass By
your tears, by the direction your hair blows

Say my name but once and turn me to stone
Say it twice and bring me back
Say it once again and watch my heart turn to sand In
your splendid hands
All of who I am and shall be

Exists between your pleasant fingers

Can we dance forever
Even beyond time
A place where the world is our band
And every garden is Eden
There will be no flaming swords for you and I Just
the chirp of the frogs on lily pad
The grasshopper tuning their violin legs
Trying to find a pitch and tone
To match the way you make love to me

My sweet morning
Covered in your golden dew
Each drop amber on a spider's web
Come sunrise
Will you make love to me this way forever
Till birds lose their song and bees forsake honey
Will you hold me this close always
Closer than the sun holds the moon
Closer than God holds her mistakes
Closer than Jesus holds his childhood
Will you kiss me this way till night comes
Wetter than a curtain made of Mary's tears
Tighter than the sky keeps each star
Can we have a love so bright
That eons after we've let this life go
It still shines for others to see
As if it were just yesterday

We can watch two fools in love
Dance in our garden
Kiss on our carpet
Make love on our bed
Point down and say
Remember when the unicorn
First called our name
And I'd slain that troll
The wizard gave us his blessing
And we gave each other our souls

The Passion of the Christ
(the lower east side version remixed)

Gabriel is tuning up
The bourbon is running low
Paul is slamming dominoes at a picnic table
John the Baptist sits on park bench in lower Manhattan
Trying to get a good signal on his cell phone
He dials hangs up dials hangs up
dials once again
On the third ring his fiancé answers
With a thick gulp of air he explains
to her how the job interview was going well when
he leapt up and exploded out the door
I'm not afraid of work, he exclaims, I just can't get used to wearing a tie
His fiancé, being a Puerto Rican born and bred
Brooklynite
simply responds
Venga tu casa papí
Tu amor está aquí
Come home my man
Your love is here

Judas watches the streetlight turn
from green to yellow to red
With a slight limp he hops out into traffic
A Jesus saves sticker is all but faded out on his purple bucket
He sloshes some dirty water on some super moms SUV and

After a few swipes she lowers her window just enough for
the dollar bill to poke out
The smile he offers her is so sincere you could almost get past
the smell
Almost

Someone starts bitching about the television playing
Oprah
Finally Mary concedes and puts the fight on
Everyone starts roaring for Joseph to open the table so he
grabs a piece of chalk from behind his ear
and stands on top of the bar
Starts taking bets
pointing at people like a trader on Wall Street
Truth be told he doesn't need the chalkboard
His memory is flawless

Jesus sits in the VIP section surrounded by women
of every shape color and creed The thing they all
talk about in the bathroom Is how he makes each
one of them feel like they are the only woman on
earth when he is with them
Whether it be conversation or more
none of them will say
Each one when asked
by another simply smiles
and turns it around saying
'Well what do you do when you're with him?'

More than anything else he likes to listen
These women come into this small hole in the wall and
talk his ear off every single night
and he listens, no matter how bad the story
He never says to leave the man
Never insists to call the cops
He never offers any advice nor does he accept their
phone numbers, he just listens

Near the bewitching hour
When his eyes begin to droop
and his mouth is full of cotton
Jesus gets up from that booth
grabs his mother's hand
and takes her out on the dance floor

Joseph, knowing his cues
jumps on top of the bar and screams
Last call for alcohol
Last call for the sweet taste of grape wine
to touch your lips and not burn
Last call for the losers and lovers
Mothers and brothers
Put down your differences
and your weapons of war
Drink one last drink with me

As always the last drink of the night is on the house
And everyone has a glass of red wine

with a salty pretzel to place on the tongue and chew
As always everyone stands in a circle
They watch Jesus dance the last dance with Mary
His head buried deep in her chest to hide his drunken sobs

All around the world they are calling
It's last call for alcohol
Someone is planning for their first child
Someone is planning for world war three
Someone is loving
Someone is leaving
Someone is talking
Someone is walking
Someone is waiting
Someone is running
Someone is screaming hallelujah
And someone is bellowing fuck you
Both of them defiant in a world gone mad
But when it's all said and done
It's still last call for alcohol

Holding his mother's hair up to his nose
Trying to take the scent with him
Once he heads out that door and up Calvary Boulevard
I heard Mary mutter, it's time to go baby
Last call for alcohol
You ain't got to go home
She said
But you got to get the hell out of here
He replied-I got to get the hell out of here

SHADOWLANDS #1

Sticks and stones may break your bones
but clichés will kill you
There is no tour bus here to speak of
When I make it back to Ohio,
the Oldsmobile will be repo'ed
faster than you can say
hey at least let me get my stuff out
or quicker than a marriage can end
Faster than the breath can leave your body
when you turn a doorknob
and are blown back against the
wall by an explosion of
complete emptiness
My last five girlfriends say I
never really got over that
Maybe they're right
Or maybe I shouldn't date carbon copies of
mistakes Quit picking hearts off of floors
then stumbling into half drunk women saying
excuse me, you dropped this

There is no manager or agent here
A mother that probably wonders
If I will ever figure shit out
A father who got me to sign off
on a life without reading the fine print

There is no theater no concert hall
No amphitheater no sold out at Madison Square Garden

No venue
Save this one right here
Which looks like the one in Toledo Smells a
bit like that one in Chattanooga The floors
squeak like the one in San Jose And I bet her
kiss tastes like New York Shit who am I
kidding
All their kisses taste like New York
New York
Not her
Not poetry
Everything I learned about love
I learned on a stage in New York
Had I listened
I would have never got married
or got that car
or that job
and I wouldn't have six broken hearts
hostage— tied up in my basement
She will love you when she chooses
It was always on her terms
She let your ego build momentum
So when it crashed and she pulled it
out of the burning wreck
She would have its undivided attention

She's never how you first see her
Never what you thought it was going
to be about
That lines about the woman
No poetry
Don't you see?

It ain't the rock star lifestyle in your head
Too much Def Poetry Jam that's what that was
She always told you to read more than your own work
(okay that lines about my ex)

No, New York
Don't you see she's more beautiful for the pain
Her leaving is what keeps you coming back
The warm February and cold June
That piss smell in the alley
Her summer's kiss
Her concrete parks beneath grumbling old trains
That's her
Her moldy words on marked up walls
That's my ex
That Hasidic cat eyeballing the hips on
that Dominican chick That's your poem
That's where she is
Your ex wife
That fluid Oldsmobile
That smile you lost somewhere in Manhattan
Then saw it buying plantains in Brooklyn
and you wonder why it wouldn't come home with you
There's your girl
All wrapped up in Coney Island
SoHo steam and laundry smoke at
four in the morning Jewish chic in
Prada pumps
A Puerto Rico flag in her nappy afro
A triple fat goosedown tied round her waist
There is your reality

So say it-
Fine:
I miss the wife in my head more than the one that left
The word New York has more uses than the word motherfucker or duct tape
Yet-
Can someone tell me why I know her kisses taste like expired metro cards
Her hair feels like asphalt dipped in honey
Why she will only argue with me in English
But intentionally says I love you in every language she knows I don't know
Why when we fight it sounds like block parties getting started
When she cums it feels like hip hop being born
Why when she walks through Central Park all the male joggers
Reach for a rib they don't have anymore
There is no glamour life in this thing
There is knowing, not knowing
The writing, not writing
The living, not living
And if you're lucky
Sometimes there's the loving
A few minutes of some stranger's time
Some scores some drinks some laughs some tears
Some time on the therapy couch
Fluid like my Oldsmobile
Cliché like the truth often is
I didn't mean to rag on you
I just saw this broken heart on the floor
thought it might be yours

She Was Section 8/He Her Only Contractor

Eyes are the windows
Mouths are the doors
Ears are the portals
The nose, a chimney
Hands are elevators
Feet are foundations
But since
that man
That
Last
Man?
He made love to her with
sledgehammers
for hands, a nail gun
for a tongue, and a jackhammer
for a dick. When he left
When
He
Left
He wrapped her in
bright yellow tape
spun from his insecurities
Took the last drops
of blood she had left
Used that ink to mark
her with one sentence
Condemned-
no date scheduled
for razing

Tarzan Rides the F Train
(Me Speak Pretty Sometimes)

You
are the
sexiest train wreck
I've ever been mutilated by
Thank you fuck you love me
tell me I'm pretty when you visit
me in the hospital stuffed full of
tubes diodes and blinking monitors
Kiss my
swollen eyes tell me
I'm pretty Help the nurse
with my bandages Hold me close
when they balance me over a
bedpan Tell me I'm pretty Feed me
ice chips Feed me
bad food
Feed me lies
Feed me
bullshit between
your kisses Never stop
feeding me kisses Walk me thru
traction Cheer me when I crawl Push me
into rehab laugh when I fall Cry when I fall
Kiss me when I fall make the pain go
away Tell me Tell me Tell me now
Tell me again Tell me
with your eyes
Tell me
with your smile
your smirk your smartass
ways Tell me with your kiss
your hug your smack your fuck
your thrust Tell me with fingernails
buried in my back bleed my fat parts trim my

lust garden Tell me with your screams as the train draws
nearer Distract me from the sound of the rotating
iron wheels Plug my nose with your musk
keep the scent of the burning coal in my
ignorant peripheral Laugh now Laugh
louder So loud I don't hear the train
hit don't hear the train crunch don't
feel the train tear don't feel the
train chew Tell me I'm
pretty sometime
Tell me I'm
pretty
Tell
me

Teddy

At two years of age Carolyn
taped a tea cup to her Teddy Bear's paw
She brewed green tea in ceremonial fashion He
accepted the ladle without speaking
As is custom, by drinking in tandem
they were married
Resting in the bottom of the cup, the leaves
warned of turbulent times ahead
Teddy saw her fear reflected in the leaves'
deadly premonition
To calm her nerves, he ate the leaves

At six years of age, Carolyn sewed a picture of
daddy between the Teddy Bear's legs
On her, Daddy called it a special place,
their sweet secret spot,
a crossroad where her baby powder
mixed with his Jack Daniel's and made a mud
of her memories
To celebrate their 4-year anniversary, Carolyn invited her
other toys and stuffed things for tea
Teddy gave Carolyn diamonds to put in her eyes
And two promises, one for each cheek
Carolyn gave Teddy a kiss

At 10 years of age Carolyn taped a bible to Teddy Bear's paw,
She had blacked out every verse of each book,
Leaving only the following passages-
*Yea though I walk through the valley on the shadow of
death I shall fear no evil*
And
Honor thy father

Carolyn figured since mommy wouldn't hear her screams and Daddy ignored her pleas to *stop touching me there it doesn't feel like love anymore*
maybe this man they call God would stop it
For their 8th anniversary Carolyn could only hug Teddy
Teddy recited *even Jesus wept* nonstop for seven days straight
then on the 8th day he became agnostic

At the age of 12 Carolyn steals her little brother's ninja man sword and tapes it to Teddy Bear's paw
thinking since prayer failed her, she could find solace in steel
Teddy had no knees or elbows, and would alternate his dreams daily between having knees to stand and walkover to the bed and cut him or elbows to perform seppuku on himself.
For their 10-year anniversary, Carolyn popped 20 children's Tylenol
Teddy regained his faith in God long enough to pray for elbows

At the age of 16, Carolyn sewed Teddy's mouth shut to muffle his screams
For their 14th anniversary, they gave each other silence.

At the age of 18, Carolyn stepped out of the bathroom from washing Daddy off

to catch Teddy plucking out his eyes because they were beautiful
Teddy ripped out all of his stuffing and filled himself with glass
Hearing of this her parents tried to throw him away, but before they could Teddy Bear stood and said "I understand
The stories that don't get told are the ones that never finish and I'm telling you now—no one will save you till you learn to save yourself."

At the age of 37, Carolyn went thrift shopping with her 2-year-old daughter
In a bin marked all items 25 cents or less
She found an eyeless Teddy Bear all but emaciated
Carolyn's eyes began to water with tears
When each one hit the pavement it turned into a diamond
Some folks called it a miracle, others ran in fear
In the house she grew up in her father slumped over dead
The police say he choked on his own tongue
The autopsy found two glass eyes and a toy ninja man sword in his stomach
At the market, Carolyn's mother was struck blind, but didn't believe it,
Claiming she could see the adults but not the children
Carolyn's daughter holds the Teddy
The moment her eyes meet Teddy's empty sockets his mouth opens and all the pages of a bible fly out
Every page blacked out, save one verse
Jesus wept
 Even Jesus wept.

The Ring

*Maxwell's never released lyrics from the bonus silence on
"Urban Hang Suite"*

This ends now. Waiter dive bombs water
replenishment, smile, a little too hard,
too long, thrusts yet another menu between
us. This plate, steamed fettuccine fogs the
wine glass, glass too cool, so hip, flasks
full of chilled whatever-his-uppity-ass-
suggested, gave a yes with mouth/get the fuck out
of here- with eyes. Glass shatters from humidity,
your hair is frizz and falling, any minute now
you'll feel a wisp tickle your ear, receive a cue,
excuse yourself.

Damn waiter is back, all twenty Hindu arms flailing,
swipes at pasta, at wine, at tablecloth, smile never
fades, never creases, plucks soggy breadstick like I'm
sure he handles his lover's post-coital limp dick,
smile twitches, promises that this won't cost me extra.
He smiles, finally makes eye contact. I left my smile
at coat check.

This tie, never knew Kenneth Cole branched out to
fashionable nooses, choking more than reassuring.
Jacket tight on the arms, didn't feel that way before I
swiped a credit card for it, shoulder pads cramping
my style. Who the fuck buys a suit with shoulder
pads still in it? Since when did I become Murphy
Brown? Does the waiter know it's 1989 only at this
table? Is that

why the reservations were so easy? I need
breadsticks that don't taste like fucking merlot.

In one more minute, she's going to smile. One
of those smiles that builds from the floor up,
through the toes and breathes out of eyelids.
What's left of the wineglass is vibrating with
the coming moment. Smile, then eyes downward,
smile, then eyes downward and grit teeth, smile,
then eyes downward and grit teeth through smile
and think 'I thought he might have been the one.'

My throat is carving the words carafe and water on its
wrists. My forehead is salivating, drooling all over my
face, asleep and dreaming of Tylenol kisses. My nose hair
is growing twice as fast as usual right now, eyelids
watching reruns of a sitcom called ' It's over now' every
time I blink.

In my jacket pocket, a box. Square, white,
single hinged box with a promise shaped like
an heirloom ring inside. A pinkie swear placed
in the mouth of an oyster a thousand years
ago, a mother's mother's mother love, protected,
prayed over, passed down and on and on, sits
in a box that apparently has had enough.

"Just take me out and place me on the table"
it says to me, this box, this lipless widemouth
priest with the snapjaw hinge, satin covered
card box for guts so old it ain't ashamed no more.

I do as I'm told, place the box on the table. The waiter straightens up, steps back two paces. The half shattered wineglass cries merlot tears, regrets not being born a chandelier. Coat check girl brings me my coat with the smile in the pocket. *"Open me up, I'll take it from here"* says the box.

I open it, slow.
Somewhere, Jesus rolls over when his lover kisses the small of his back. Icarus makes love to the Sun behind the guise of clouds, a girl with a mouth full of braces locks lips with a boy at prom, his cut lip just a rite of passage,
and this...woman, her eyes, her nose, the sudden rise and fall and rise of her breasts, her pulse
I can hear like a siren song, blood thick, true, and dazzling to the ear, this constant yearning across the table from me, all of her says what her mouth can't find form, what I couldn't find to say.

God Made Dirt and Dirt Don't Hurt

I.
Snatch the pebble from my hand
name it heart
Steal my breath away with a smile
name it happy
Make me forget for a moment who I am
name it time

II.
There is a mood indigo
which no longer wishes to be
so blue
A color beyond the
comforting touch
of rainbows
She wishes for proper names
Here. Now. Before. After. Later. She
only winds up with tendrils of clouds
vaportwisting in the wind

III.
Once, I held a Sunday in my hand
It felt nothing like holy,
nothing like righteous
until I did what most children do
(put it in my pocket)
forgot about it
Till the summer heat had melted
whatever form it once held

IV.
My mother's smile was built
on the backs of plumbers, construction working
men; fellows whose spines knew the language
of the unforgiven Her breath was stitched of
canaries that never made it back to the surface
(her sighs just so many whistles combined)

V.
She calls me to her side
Hands me the pants
from the summer before
fresh out the dryer
Inside the front left pocket
the washed, dried, melted remnants
of a Sunday I had long since forgotten

VI.
Canaries become eagles
in the throat of a mother
Summers become blinks
in the mind of a child
But Sundays?
Sundays become holier when forgotten, set
aside, washed, dried, melted and placed in the
hands of a child

VII.
God created
the three-second rule
Sometimes we get dropped
But then, if you wait for it a
breeze soft and yellow ruffles
your hair and suddenly
you're good again.

Paul's Purgatory Walk to the Lonesome Valley

You got to go to the lonesome valley
You got to go there by yourself
Nobody else can go for you
You got to go by yourself

Thunderclap
African woman walking down Van Buren
Skin darker than my nightmares Bus ride
wheels spin on overpass

Dirt on my face
Sunshine smacks off the back of a shovel
and I'm Lonesome Valley bound

Remind me again momma
where'd I misplace my youth
Father
Where's your voice
like a rainstorm to wash my way clear

Lord there's a man on the bus
with no tomorrow in his eyes and he looks like me

You got to go to the Lonesome
Valley
7th Avenue brickyard entrance
offers no reprieve
Maricopa chain gang shake
shackles like tambourines

All the trees sway as if to avoid my touch

More dirt on my face

Lonesome Valley, I rebuke your kiss
your touch, your tender lovemaking
Where are my shining rivers and fat fish
Granmama got chitlins simmering now like
the intestines of a slaughtered God

Am I not a conqueror
Am I not a God
Is my skin not a mighty armor
keeping your hell hounds at bay
Don't I deserve a seat at the victor's table

It wasn't me who knocked the cup over
spilled the holy wine
Let me keep my blood and I'll let you keep yours
Why's that noose whispering my name
Why's that tree branch smiling at me

Thunderclap

Somewhere there's a woman
with child bearing hips fretting
over a hot stove You kiss her
for me now Use your softest
touch Tell her the thunder
and rain are hers to keep
I'm Lonesome Valley bound

"Ed Mabrey has figured out what he wants to say and is becoming increasingly more adept at the *how* of it. The voice of his poems is a sure one, inventive in its tone and celebratory in all its breadth. These poems seek to reach out and confirm their composer as a reckoning in the world he inhabits. He pushes the throat of them through you. He will not be denied. These poems will not sit still."

Roger Bonair Agard
National Individual Poetry Slam Champion
Cave Canem Alum

Juno Se Mama

In a part of Africa known as Darfur, thousands of men have stormed the country and killed almost all of the men and some of the boy children. They proceeded to rape every woman they could get their hands on. They storm the area whenever they please and have turned an entire people into a brothel that charges no fee.

Dear women of Darfur,
I am sending you a package
It has not been paid in advance
It is not fragile
It is stronger than the cardboard that holds it
It does not matter which way it is turned
No precious parts will be broken
You will need no instructions
No one need sign for it
The package knows you
Women of Darfur
I am sending my mother
Her name changes with the wind
But she will insist, call her Phyllis

In the second box, you will find
my old Bronco Billy cowhide leather belt
with the big rodeo buckle made of brass
It will look like a Texas snake with hell on
its' mind, don't worry
It will not strike, nor raise its head in warning
The instructions in this box are just one-
Place the belt in her hand
Point her toward these men who rape you
Then, for your own good

get the hell out of her way

Dear men of Darfur,
loosely translated, you call yourselves
men on horses of death carrying guns
My mother will enjoy that
She will tell you to keep the horses
I will warn you to keep your guns
I am afraid the death will be all hers

The belt is fusing in her hand
becoming one with her flesh
digging until it finds blood
tasting hers it awakens
A tornado in her hand
The kraken clasped in her fist
And her war cry sounds like
the ripped hymen of Winnie Mandela

Where are your bullets now?
She eats them like memories
When my father called her bitch
and made her smile
When a deacon called her love
and left money on the dresser
When a pastor raised her skirt
When a mugger punched her pregnant womb

Bring on your horses Watch as
they buck, stomp chomp at their
bits to get away

Animals know the scent of natural disaster
and Phyllis is on her way with dust devils for
breasts razors for labia she drank the oceans of
this world and holds them inside begging you
to rape her and drown when her water breaks

We will find the graves of your mothers
make spoons from their bones stretch their
skins for drums
We will not abort these seeds you planted
We will feed them kernels of your history
Teach them songs of how they came to be
They will dance till their feet bleed into thirsty earth

Dear Children of Darfur, do not fret.
My mother will teach you to make spears of your
mothers bones, rattles from their teeth, feathers from
their eyelashes.
You will go by no name that isn't muttered in the
deathblow of one of your fathers.

The woman with lightning for hair,
giraffes for arms, elephants for breasts,
and cheetahs for feet, goes by many names,
Phyllis, mother, righteous vindicator, even Africa,
But she will insist, call her by her proper name—
The right hand of Darfur.
The left hand of God.
I send you this package c.o.d.
Use your fathers'
 skulls and blood as payment.

THE MAIL TRAIN

Séance

President Obama fell into a mysterious coma today. In his right hand was a note on how to speak to the dead…

   I.
Malcolm Speaks
I gave up pimping for you Found
God during a block party and we
made love on 125th St.
I have bullet wounds shaped like
crescent moons and eastern stars
These tattoos I give to you freely
Bring me the fat from
Al Sharpton and Thurgood Marshall
Make me a candle

   II.
Run Jesse Run
First base rhymer
Second base liar
Third base marching with Martin cause
You heard the news cameras would be there
Doesn't give you a lifetime pass

You gotta hit a homerun Jesse
Run Jesse
Hymietown Harlem homerun hitter
Kiss your fingers twice
Point at the nosebleed seats
And swing one for child support

Look into the light, cry blinding tears
Sambo your Stephen Biko impersonation
While your eyes tantrum
It could've been me

III.
Dream of Californication (x4)

IV.
Gary Coleman, Sammy Davis Jr., Mr. Bojangles Nipsy
Russell, Robert Guillaume, Nell Carter, The entire
Cast of *Good Times*, George Jefferson, his wife, maid
And children all go to the Million Man March in new
Track shoes, stopwatches, and uzi's for starter pistols

V.
Cash Rules Everything Around Me, C.R.E.A.M.- get
the money, dollar dollar bill y'all

VI.
The blocked number that keeps calling you Obama Then
hanging up belongs to Coretta Scott King

VII.
When asked how it feels to have the most red states turn
blue in a presidential race ever, John McCain replied,
"Like a black man."

VIII.

And the machine guns Jimi, and the machine guns
Jimi, And the guns, and the guns, and the guns

IX

Wake up democratic Aladdin
Ride your magical carpetbag carpet over this land you control
We the people are an evil Jafar
Save us from ourselves

X.

Nelson Mandela Fuses with Nikki Giovanni
It is not that we are afraid of being inadequate
Nigga can you kill
It is we are afraid of being powerful
Nigga can you kill

XI.

Malcolm Speaks Again
Make the White House a mosque
Take the family for walks around it seven times a day
They will come for you armed with smiles and promises
When you lose focus, do not think of what they did to Emmett or Medgar
Remember what they did to Rwanda and Russia Pakistan and Indo-China

Keep your teeth polished and hide bombs in your grin
Remember anytime the words Black and Leader

Are placed next to each other They
click like a bullet in a chamber

You can call me, Barack Call me
anytime you need me to come back Kiss
your wife for me, have you ever noticed
your daughters have my eyes

"Ed is what racist security guards would call 'the good one'. He's a horn in the wilderness of the poetry scene, whose professional attitude and unique talent have placed him in the tradition of artists like Umar and Patricia, who enhance the humble art of delivering human being (in all its definitions) through microphones. I met him when I was a freshman in college still trying to put two good lines together. Back when I had one solid poem that just so happened to be about Bruce Lee, he was the only person who got the jokes. He gave many formerly voiceless artists like myself a space called Black Pearl Poetry that reflected his own admiration of the craft: "let the words speak for themselves." A life-changer, a satirist, a theatre craftsman, a page/stage orchestrator, a reverberation, and a heart like an orange, Mr. Mabrey has a contagious sense of adventure and ear for honest business. He also has the irrational talent of finding ice cream: dude can get some vanilla ice cream in a rain forest during storm-season with a x-men t-shirt on Christmas day. A courageous mentor, dangerous competitor, an even better friend; Ed has given a lot of people a thumbs up and a hug in a scene in which both are necessary and rare and has done so effortlessly with a vision of the world that could pretty much paint ceilings."

Dave Nichols
-poetry participant

In The Name of Our Father

for Dave Nichols and Roger Bonair-Agard after watching "City of God"

Rainbows can be frozen
in the City of God
where dogs are kings
Reefer smoke does not
require an r.s.v.p. from
your nostrils your lungs
to flood your veins
and there are more shell
casings from guns on
the ground than there are
children's feet to step on
them where dogs are kings

You grow up with a
machete in your baby
fist Calloused thumbs
from wheelbarrows
full of fish to sell that
you push all day Suck
on those digits they are
your only pacifier Milk
is stolen from goats or
cows stolen from neigh-
boring slum stolen from
lot where old women
lay dead splayed out
in final prayer over her
prideful husband both

of them dead by your
gun your bullets your
hands where the dogs
are kings

Tourists love you for your
smiles and constant laughter
musíca musíca they call it Ask
you to dance in street make
your smile dance can you make
your smile dance there is no
gold in your tooth but there is
money in your smile now dance
Look at them looking at you
white skin red with a sun's kiss
your skin black with the
knowing with the power of the
words yes no and death
Remember even the sun is a
traitor at noon falling with favor
anyone one who sits on his
beaches make love in his sand
spend money at tourist traps run
home tell friends of *the great
time they had you must come
with us next time look at
pictures developed watch 8mm
film shaky in rum soaked hand
we found this bronze this taupe
this french vanilla this
butterscotch*

*this dark this dark this dark this
pitch black this smooth black
this panther this black panther
this dark cougar this foreign
negro this boy this boy this boy
this darling of a little boy with
skin like the ocean shimmering
shimmering a evil blue black we
found this kid gave him
money and he danced laughed
smiled he danced smiled laughed
he danced for us in the street
kicked up dirt for us in the shit
put on quite the show never
stopped smiling for us he
danced for money* where the
stray dogs are all kings

We hood We hoodlums and
unpaved streets slum towns with no
electricity no parliament We jump
gas trucks like your kids jump non-
smoking ashtrays couch cushions
smash piggy banks in summer time
for bum rushing the ice cream man
the Italian ice man We shoot
bullets at driver never caring
about his cargo exploding We
laugh as he protects the boss
mans money more bullets at his
feet make him dance jig

make him smile Our smiles never leave our faces as we rob we kill we shoot we maim Our laughter keeps you alive sometimes keeps us sane some times keep us going sometimes We smack you if your hands fly up in surrender We respect you if you keep them by your side even while you piss your pants relief yourself are betrayed by your bladder your body we respect your heart and piss never hurt anyone this place is our home our refuge our battle ground our sewer Our sewage gets sunburns and fades fast enough into the dirt Only the gods will know you were there and will piss over yours to mark to claim to stake sovereign again this cracked and bleeding earth where the dogs are kings

She looks at me you know Your lady your lover your wife Wants me my smile my accent my foreign negro ways Can't decide which shade of me to taste The fair skinned with dirty blonde hair Can't be a nigger The

white skinned with red hair and
freckles peeking from the waistline
of his shorts Can't be a nigger The
cafe au lait now a burnt and seeth-
ing bronze like Aries in the nude
Can't be a nigger The dark one like
a tiger a puma a great jungle beast
rising on two feet walking like the
rest of us up right skin a polished
ebony mirror reflecting all my lusts
in each rippling muscle a body alive
like I have never seen Can't be a
nigger

It is your name she lets loose from
the bowels of her uncharted pits
tombs and waters says it in English
doesn't think I understand this
language I don't need to know your
dialect to know when another
man's name is being called from
beneath me in the slums my slums
You will leave me some money a
tennis bracelet to give to my mother
I will sell it instead mama's been
dead for years now and your
leftover chicken from the chicken
man's truck This I will give to the
dog

outside this room The one you are
afraid of He looks too ragged too tired
to live much less bark You can count
his ribs if you took the time Notice
how no one teases him No one kicks
dirt in his face Everyone gives him
plenty of room to pass where ever he
wants to go I will give him your
leftover chicken as a thanks a token a
gift a tithe a sacrifice to his godness
on this street where the dogs are kings

Tonight you will leave me
All of you The gay priest
and his exclamations of faggot
every ten seconds every thrust
every jowl shaking push he
made into the little boys here
the ones with long hair and soft
voices who take the money to their
mothers their grand mothers wash
their hair and dip the ends in
peroxide make the blonde out of
black You will leave me teenage
girl take with you my reefer my
cocaine even now sings songs to
you blue songs pretty songs happy
songs Songs that can blot out the
entire world for minutes

hours days soon won't be enough to
blot out the song the songstress she
sings pretty songs in key veins and
arterial motives lit by supply and
demand should've bought the old
man's sugarcane treats maybe and icee
but you were so eager so eager to grow
up to learn to understand why parents
look so bitter You will leave me
woman with your sated lust Will you
think of me in nine months

You will leave me Man of hers You
will want to forget my face after the
tenth friend neighbor golf buddy asks
to see the photos see the slides see the
film of the dancing boy in the street
You will smile and say sure wondering
if they want to see me or watch your
wife dance with me

And you You can't stop seeing me In
your lemonade in your summer in your
heat and dog day afternoons in your
cool refrigerator back in the corner You
dig for me wrist deep in the black
forbidding spaces of your garbage
disposal your ice cream man winks your
milkman's

weather advice your cold dead
television late at night that watches
you with an all seeing glare Even in
your mirror but most of all in smiles In
smiles you will see me frozen in every
photo every family portrait from now
on Your smile frozen filled with every
color
like a rainbow Like a rainbow
high on reefer smoke Like a
rainbow on vacation from the
good life come to paradise to see
what heaven looks like
what heaven feels like what heaven smells
like what heaven taste like Only to get
there Only to get here and discover that
heaven has no sidewalks no running water
Heaven has no electricity Heaven has
more bullets in it than children's playful
feet Your God left heaven a long time ago
And now heaven belongs to
the dogs Where the stray dogs are king

Heart of Steel

(for Dave Nichols & Jim Dwyer & Shappy & Jerry Humphrey)

That was my Dayton you took in your autumn with breath full of peaches out of season. I can't get high off this city, this slick, this cock-less master, this constant surge protector, blocks me from voltage, from charge, from contact made brutal on streets called Dixie and Poe, Prescott and Gettysburg. And while on the subject, how and where was your name planted on my seed, this concrete I tilled for years made only of winters and snapped snow shovels? When did your breath plume a smoke signal, what message did you pen from the steam escaping your nappy head in the blizzard of '78?
Let me see the graveyard marker for your ghetto snowman, made from more stone than snow, more sludge and grit then Christmas. And what of your mothers?
Bring me their matted, grey hair, the permanently down turned mouths, mouths too full of " I'm Sorry's" and "Maybe next time's", too bloated with repressed screams to give smiles on most days.

What tree did you plant brother? In my city? Did you smoke skunk weed with Clayton? Did you watch his crossover? His finger roll? Did you cry? Did you run home in high shorts and knees high socks and drag out that warped basketball with the titty on it bigger than Melissa Parker's? Did you practice day and night? Did your tears make you grow tall enough to dunk? To touch the rim like Jesus touched the sun in his child years?

Did you feel his arms around you, strong like your absent fathers promises, broken for so long you can't recall if they were ever real, ever true, ever a promise?

Did you find Clayton with the yellow skin
and naturally curly afro in the parking lot, on his side, on his side not breathing, smelling like the water in your excuse for a town river, needle still in his arm? Did you touch the face, that pretty peach fuzz face, almost wish him back, almost offer your ten-year-old soul as a bribe for a God who'd already moved on to more important, shiny, living things? Did you feel the phantom twitch of the needle when you pulled it out? Was it a shoebox or your old Operation game that you stashed it in? Did you visit the body four days later, when it was bloated and black, black like your skin, your miserable black skin, your detestable black skin, did you hate black skin that spring, like a tomb out in the open did you walk along the River Styx, listening to the winos doo-wop testimonials? Did you play ball Saturday after the dump truck came and got the body, not a body anymore, just a smell, a funk, a rotted horse from your past, a make believe thing, an urban legend, Clayton the wonderful what, the incredible who, the forever shrinking half man-half forgotten? Did you win every game you played? Crossover so fast you left your own fat behind? Did Melissa Parker fall in love with you for ten points, a round of 21, did you spot boys bigger than you points, give a head nod when they asked if they could run with you? Did you choke on your own tongue

when the alley opened up for you, pick up left foot, one hundred eighty degree turn, pivot on right, feint weight to left thigh, push ball through legs, back into same hand, complete spin and leave the earth behind one step in from the foul line?

Did the air up there smell like Honeybuns? Elevate nigga, higher fatboy. Yes. Hook's BBQ is the smell of every outdoor basketball net-less rim. Then, without warning or permission did Clayton show up, like Jesus with holes in hands and feet, brandishing the very sword he'd been pierced with? Didn't Clayton's smell kiss your finger roll? Wasn't the ball just a pumpkin from last years Trick or Treat, an onion brown and black hiding in the back of Nana's cupboard, rabid and rancid with ignorance and pain, the venom that only comes from a thing so easily forgotten?

Was it you who ran home trailing snot and tears and spit in his wake? Ashy knees on shag carpet, Clayton's needle in your hand, arm high and tremble tight, basketball clinched between your legs? Then the blow, puncture, stab, wrench free, raise, scream, strike. Curse a deaf God, stab, wrench free, suck breath like you stole it from the Van Dykes. Who did you see in the basketball's Wilson reflection? Was it your father not father? Your mother tired mother? Or was it your high yellow Nana with the pretty hair? Hair like Clayton's?
Did you puncture her lung in one of those blows? Are you that man, brother? Was it Cleadie, the man you never called grandfather, with skin darker than your

dreams, darker than the corpse of what's-his-name-with-the-good-finger roll?

Was it for one minute you own face?

Did you fight in piles of leaves in other folks' yards?
Make
pinkie swears, blood oaths with pocketknives stolen from Elder
Beerman's? How many chumps you hustle at Dixie pool hall?
Did the wrinkled white man whose sweat tastes like Pabst Blue
Ribbon and death buy you a cheeseburger?
Exclaim he ain't never met a nigger he wouldn't rather shoot
than save but goddamn if you didn't have a smile that
reminded him he had kids once, somewhere, sometime,
some cities and demons ago. Did he teach you to play
snooker? Explain if you can, make love to the small pockets
you can fuck'em in the big ones? You ever roll them
bones?
Chalk'em, rack'em boy, loser buys the onion chips and the
next pack of lucky shorts, unfiltered. What you know about
twelve hours with no break, no rest, and that first and last
cigarette, given to you by another fool in the green room
between sticks and cues, that outside wind, cold and honest,
making the inhalation of crop dusted plantation tobacco all the
sweeter for a moment, that deep flame sucking in your lungs,
virgin lungs fucking a poison with a big dick for a time.

Till he came out and saw you. Caught you by your arm and
smacked the fire from your mouth. "Don't ever let me see
you with that shit in your mouth." he warned and swelled up
to swing, to fight, to engage your niggerdom like a creed, and
before you could muster bravado, he smacks you again,
till you can see outside the tears and can't breathe beyond the
gasp and pause. Did you tell him he wasn't your father,
your papa, your daddy, tell him to go fuck himself? Did you
hear when he said he was already fucked and would
rather see your black ass dead then go the route he'd
already went? Did the warning sound like love, love you
never knew you had lost somewhere in the womb,
somewhere in the Cincinnati escape artists trickery of the
man who bore you? Did you weep?
Did you think Dayton was just a hometown?

"Ed Mabrey compels me to reenlist in Gentleman Practice 101 every single time I'm in his presence. His words come from giant wells of breathtakers and bomb water, good graces and paradigm wrecking balls. His edge is near invisible, the kind that cuts right through the bullshit and down to the heart strings before you know you've even bled."
-Buddy Wakefield
Two time Individual World Poetry Slam Champion

"Mabrey's vast gift is instantly apparent to the listener. His writing is rain forest thick, while his voice brings to mind a tenor like tonality. He bleeds ink".

-- Taalam Acey

"I love being in the room when Ed Mabrey's got the microphone. On stage, his commitment to the artform truly comes through in both his writing and his performance; you can tell that he is constantly reaching for something deeper than the applause. My fondest memories of Ed, though, are away from the stage (where he sounds remarkably like Gilbert Gottfried, by the way).

No microphones, no competition, just two guys sharing a meal and some bullshit. Ed Mabrey is an excellent bullshitter and an even better friend. What can I say? I like the cat."

--J.W. Baz; Writer/Performer, 2007 IWPS Finalist

Marrow

The rose
in the vase
on table
by her bed
is fatter
than she is.

Cancer has a
many mouthed
soul, each one
never graduated
past gluttony
in the school
for deadly sins.

Mother's Milk

(headnod to Will Evans)

for Kanye West after the passing of his mother from plastic surgery complications

Do you still think of her breasts?
Do you ever see the babies?
Babies of babies
babies with babies,
those tireless, motherless mothers?
Mothers without mothers of babies in
tow, under arm, on hip
like dope boys tote glocks on the
Southside, your side, do they
catch your shaded eye?

Have they run into you
in alleys, cornered you,
babies in hand, glocks,
weapons with bullets
as teeth, trigger safeties
for pacifiers

Diapers made from their G.E.D.'s,
from their WIC coupons, from their
Section 8 vouchers, Similac labels,
black & white generic labels, strollers
constructed from front door drop
powdered milk, and condensed milk,
and regular milk for the lucky on
Lenox, on Quinton, on Rosemore,

diapers made from 1.4, from 2.2,
from 2.5 GPA, from failed AIMS
test, from letters written by once
good guidance counselors, now
dead paperweights holding down
jobs and federal funding, notes
which read, "no hope", and "seek a
trade", and "best suited to work
with her hands"

Might as well say-
lie down for boys
spread legs
make babies
abort babies
make babies
make more babies
work with your hands
stay in bed
stay on corner
stay in street
stay in ghetto
covet thy project
castrate your roses
worship this concrete

college is a foreign word
university, a distant land
happiness, a false god
success, a golden calf
bow before entering

your corner store
pour a little out for yourself
make babies
stay on your knees

These girls, Kanye
These glock-baby
toting women
Have you been pinned in
a corner with them, holding babies
whose knitted eyebrows spell your
mother's name, have they looked
upon you with dead eyes, eyes
which think Michigan Ave. is a
myth, have they ripped open their
shirts and showed you their filthy
breasts, hollow angles, deep
sockets of no flesh, absent nipples,
sackcloth for cleavage, in fact,
nothing at all beneath those shirts
except for a tired three-legged dog
for a heart, too tired to go on
running, too tired to lie down and
die?

Who will feed our babies now
is what they ask you, as babies
slink out of their grasps
and crawl towards you, ooze
towards you, grabbing pants leg,
snagging belt loop, climbing over

one another towards your chest,
your Kanye source, your K-Yeezy,
source of your impotent swagger
and malevolent cocktease, rip
your shirt to shreds, open their
little mouths to a sickening degree,
jaws creaking out your latest song,
precious little mouths filled with
row after row of bullet teeth,
diamond teeth, platinum teeth,
gold fronts with your name on them,
now suck your nipples Kanye,
since mother cut hers off, they will
suck till they drink your hits, your
misses, your bootlegs and b-sides,
your hard work torn asunder, suck,
your mohawked frivolity, suck, your
key to the city, suck, give us your
milk they cry, we are a hungry brood
with no mother to feed us, feed us
your sizzle shit K-Yeezy, teach us
swagga-no-swagga, sing us lullabies
of the one you took from us
with practiced nonchalance,
our mouths are your remix, our
thirst-your hook

Have you ran into these women, these
babies, Kanye?
Have they found you out yet?

I'm curious, I heard a scream in the
breeze last night woke me out of
sleep, chilled me to the bone
Only Chicago has wind like that
Was it you Kanye?
Was it you I heard screaming
in the breeze?

In the Wake of the Shadow

Her hand, white
The teacup trembles
on its saucer

The door

opens

Hinges creak a
small warning
of his approach

Her back
is turned

The door

closes

Coat hung on peg
in front room

Mud caked boots
kicked off
in foyer

Sleeves rolled up
in hallway

In the kitchen
a shadow

grows
on her back
eclipses the sun

A calloused hand
rises toward
the sky

On the floor
the saucer
spins and dances

The teacup sits
in pieces
Watches
the liquid
once inside it
move
across the floor
like blood

A Pocketknife is not a Plaything: Instructions for my Son

Plant a tree. Find a spot green, a spot true. Plant a
green truth. Bury every promise with that seed,
every hope, fear, regret, every little dust mote
you caught spying in the highway of a sunbeam
through a bathroom window.

Nurture your tears so that they might grow
strong and have respect for the faces upon
which they travel. Teach tears the inner
meaning of moisture, of locked lips and
intimate passions that rebuke pink.
Make them respect that color, pink.

Smile a sunbeam, a mouthful of sunbeams.
Photosynthesize this backyard, this ghetto, this
bubblegum on concrete, this hot summer, this ice
cream, both truck song and promise. Add heat to that
jingling bell. Listen for the rakes, ten of hundreds of
tiny fingers scraping couch seat cushions, the mouths of
old cigarette ashtrays, dusty and accepting of change,
bottoms of momma's purses, with and without
permission, raking the swift demise of piggy banks,
hammer on ceramic pork explosions, plaster of Paris
everywhere, your hands, your hair (so nappy), your
eyes. All those coins, a bridge, a noisy bulge, a contract
between children and summer, forever.

By now, you have forgotten the pocketknife
the old man gave you and the tree out back. Go to
them both. Introduce yourself to them as you would
to future in-laws. Watch the tree pull up her skirt so
that you may see she already knows you. In her thigh,
your initials from years ago. Beneath them, a blank
space encircled by a heart. Dig into her leg boy, carve
the name of the one you want, leave initials like
morse code.

Pay tithes to the tree, the yard, and the swing
that is not a swing, the nosy neighbor across bushes, and
the golden collie that never barks at you,
a reincarnated watchman. Pay with your belief, your
sweat, carvings, those approaching curves.

Trust she will come to you, smelling of summer rain and
frustration penned up too long. Trust she will know the whip of
grass against soft skin, the burn, honestly sweet, trust she will
have a smile like double dutch, dangerous and inviting. In her
hand, she'll grip a dirty pocketknife, more rust than real. Her
chest holds a block of wood embedded, heart-shaped, with
initials. Her smile, a tingling bell and sunbeams, enough to eat
for days.

Pugilism, Round One:
Che Guevara vs. Biggie Smalls

from **the upcoming Pugilism: The War of Art**

Your Jehovah wears images of me
with rhyming African musicians as his backdrop increasing
status of street credential with my eyes gazing out from
rhinestoned cotton
Funny, for I rarely liked to look at myself
So you know my exterior better than I
And I know your soul
Or at least the fire ravaged forest
where your spirit ran free

I went from three hots and a cot
To three-tiered yachts
From bitches who burned cuz they was hot
To bitches who burn cuz they hot
So dope I use samples of my samples
For my next sample example
Birthdays was the worst days
now we sip champagne when we thirsty

I come from men who measure their age
by how many hang from the town square noose
What do you know of machete-callused hands
What you call body counts and death tolls,
we call a lazy Sunday afternoon; a good day to
pray to a angry God for justice
so the eagle might find music in its wings and
the dove grow talons

Nigga, please,
I put Brooklyn on the map
snapped my fingers and like
that The whole world was my
audience Listen to them clap

Show me this real estate you own
Take me to the tree your grandfather planted so
his future wife would have shade
and his children swings and food
Bring to me a clump of this earth that
bears your signature
Find me one of these niggas that
recognizes you by your smile

It used to take me days to get
bitches now I got bitches for days
Used to steal to get my weed
now I smoke sticky green in purple haze
Remember multiplatinum status last
forever You just some cat in a funny-
shaped hat Don't make me pull the gat or
have my boys Martinize ya no go run tell
dat Who shot ya?

My dear black Jesus
Was it the hashish that blinded you at the dinner table When
you reached for your cup did you not feel a hand of another
graze your own
Was it your friends who left Jerusalem
before your imminent crucifixion

Were they the ones who woke in terror sweats,
blood on their hands
For all your rhyming did you so easily forget your
Shakespeare, the only bitch I have ever met was named
Macbeth and last I saw of her off paper was when she
was in your arms in a video

I got soldiers that sling boulders
from Charlotte To Boulder, Colorado.
Crisp tees & pop collars like raw
dough
We hit Cuba for cigars and Miami Beach for raw
hoes You only speak of hardcore
I got Mac 10's stashed in the dog pen and
a.k.'s in secret compartments in the hallway
Pissed me off I got the sawed off
so when they bury you it'll be a little casket
cuz Your torso's sawed off
We don't get down we go off
in the street they call me stainless cuz I'm never soft

Have you looked in the eyes of a 12-year-old boy and
reminded him that his death furthers revolution Did you
sleep well the night he marched away armed with a gun, a
knife, and a flag for a cape
Have you murdered dreams just to keep your hope I
came in this world a surgeon and leave as one
I gave a continent mouth-to-mouth resuscitation and
an America an enema that was long overdue

Duke the Moon

semi lit alleyway
2:37 in the a.m.
red/blue battle
for space on walls

checklist-
one blue dumpster
lid thrown back
like rigamortis lockjaw

one three legged dog
doesn't flinch or stop
eating leftover sandwich

two graffiti tags
Brooklyn Forever
on the right
Danielle loves Manny

one shoe, still laced all
the way up, lies on its
side, twenty feet from
anything

blood, forming three rivers
one snakes towards the wall
as if trying to put as much
space between it and what
happened, another eases
toward the party of cock-
roaches, the last puddles

close to its former master,
hoping to find a way back in

somewhere in this alley
there are spent casings,
smoke still clings to the air.

beneath the boy's jacket, five
holes. His necklace is gone,
and his stash. Even the
diamond & gold fronts are
gone, leaving only an
immaculately polished white
smile.

"Watching the unflappable Mr. Mabrey take administrative, strategic and creative charge of a room of sweaty and increasingly irritable black folk when the air conditioning in his venue refused to budge. He managed to keep things under control with a potent mix of charm, competence and humor--and he spat a few kickass poems besides.

Mabrey is a gale force on the poetry scene (not just the SLAM poetry scene), constantly setting up new challenges in his work, and constantly knocking them down for the next new thing."

Patricia Smith
Winner of the National Poetry Series and the Hurston-Wright Award in Poetry, Cave Canem and Stonecoast MFA faculty, former National Poetry Slam champion

"When I first head Ed Mabrey, I called him The Voice of God, like everyone else; it wasn't until his words had sunk in, however, that I realized he had been touched by Her as well."

Taylor Mali
HBO Def Jam Poet, Educator, National Slam Champion

Collette Sims

for Mo Browne, Dasha Kelly, Patricia Smith, and my Mother

I.
The little girl
on the left
picks the white doll
up
places it down
picks up the black doll
places it down
then is handed a mirror
"What do you see?"
she is asked
"Who are you?"
she is asked
"Which one are you?"

II.
When asked
how she felt
about wearing
blackface
Judy Garland
replied, *"invigorated."*

III.
It is rumored
that when asked
why The Blues
were called
The Blues,

Muddy Waters replied-
"To call the music
the Blacks
would be redundant."

IV.
The little girl on the right
unsheathes a pocketknife
and cuts the heads off both dolls She
says neither resemble her
(She later ran for President)

It was a full eight hours
before the girl on the left
answered
V.
When she stood up
she had grown
two feet taller
(making her a full six feet even)
Her smile peeled open
like a ripe banana
at a Jamaican stand
Her mouth opened
until it appeared it would
come unhinged at the joint
From her gaping maw
another woman came forth
crawled right out of her head,
then another
and another

and another
till the room was filled with
little women girls Then the little
girl (four-foot Norman
Rockwell of a Negro girl child)
spoke up

VI.
You ask what I resemble
I resemble Harlem at 3 a.m. in
1945 and Nagasaki in '52 My
hair was braided by dead
African mermaids tethered to
the ocean floor by kelp
shackles I use clouds for
earrings and mountains for
medallions I am the brown
skinned nanny whose teat you
suckled in the cold months and
the master's wife who clutched
her breasts in despair and
shame

VII.
I am unflinching in my judgments

VIII.
I am Bethsheba and Ruth
I hold King Solomon's Mines
between my toes and your oceans in
my womb

I get pregnant off laughter
and orgasm from your wars

IX.
I make you dance for me

X.
I am the maid that dusts the chamber of
Walt Disney's frozen corpse
I am Minnie Mouse smoking meth in
Parking Lot B on her lunch break

I am Coretta Scott King
cashing that first Coca Cola check
with a steady hand

XI.
My right hand smacked
the face of Jesus when
he brought home bad grades or
broke my favorite dish

I severed the penis of Ra because he
wasn't working it right I made you
eighty percent water so my oceans
could always drown you

I am Shiva of Death
the bright morning star
I am all things that point East
I am the one who found the stone rolled

away and found your Jesus just so
He might find himself in me again
I wear constellations as hip chains
and dwarf stars for chastity belts

XII.
All my decisions are final
I do not take refunds
I never apologize
My lips hold every sin
and my kiss every salvation
and you fools ask me which doll?

XIII.
You can no more define me by
black and white
then you can define the night by
the depth of its shade

With that said,
the little girl
opened her mouth
one last time
and roared.

A Hero's Welcome: Richard Pryor on His Way Home from the Motherland

A failure, fuck-up,
red-headed stepchild of a
devil drunk on senility,
former husband of the
nursemaid whom dipped
Achilles' body, but didn't
protect his soul, an accident,
an aborted abortion, some
half envisioned thing, still
wet and warm, a half
cooked mold of
a man, left in the kiln too long
by a simian too busy placating
Jesus and lesser sun-gods,
something better forgotten, but
impossible to let go, dancing a
mangled leg
jig in the dust bunny corners of
your mind's bed, kicking up
dust, ether, funk,
and smiles half stabbed, left for
dead, this potent mildew, this
winged malaria, a fever of
bones, shat from the mouth of
the mountain that made Judas'
metal coins,

a blacksmith too long in the deep, more
mole than man, a sniveling thing, with
whiskers, and snout, snorting worm shit
like cocaine, belly full of what weeds
excrete and leave behind when done
wiping their asses with rose petals,
tulips, whatever dream you dared to
share with them, spoke your secrets into
some filthy hole, covered it and thought
it done, complete. You feel foolish now
watching them, but you watch. That is
your penalty. Watch them chew your
bubblegum til it grows black, black in
the negative connotation of the elders
and slave owners, black with fear, black
with pride, with power,

so much power in the black, with its
continent for a cock. Nations eager to
suckle its golden breasts that house many-
lipped nipples, asking for passwords,
answers, sphinx, for return to sender, for
daughters turned dust, for forty acres
burned, save the sugarcane, and mules
gutted, split open, cooked over open pits
and cured for jerky, food for the long haul
back, back to the first class private jet seat,
back to the afro, the jheri curl,

manicured nails, custom suits, back to jim brown
in lowercase lifestyle, back to millionaire
activism, back to step-but-never-fetch, never
retrieve, never retrieve what you lost. You lost.
They lost, we lost, all that we lost in that most
holy of fire walkers, you with a free-based pipe
for a crown and Sunset Strip for a Gethsemane,
hollywood, a lowercase Damascus, and you, king
of kings, lord of lords, white powder on your
nose, white woman on your side, scream black
power! Scream free Mumia! Scream R-E-S-P-E-
C-T! Scream Rutgers, scream Tuskegee, Scream
Chicago, Scream Mudbone!

No, whisper the last one, lest you wake the giant,
the real, the now, the here, the fuck you, the
caricature with Huey P. Newton's face, too late.
He awakens on Broadway, big enough to swallow
your America, your needles, your clap, your beret,
your militia, your junta, your C.I.A., your lack of
proof. Here is your anomaly back from a dead that
never was to swallow you whole, ask you to show
him what Africa you left behind which Africa did
you bring home with you? The one with the
distended belly, or the tour-guided giraffe?
Tanzania, was she there? Did Zimbabwe check
bags underneath or

pack its death in a carry-on? Did you notice
them sneaking on the plane? See the pygmy
in the back stealing glances
at your white woman, curious and aroused, both of
them wanting to conquer something smaller and
bigger than themselves? Didn't Jim Brown look a
little like Mandela, slumped drunk in his chair, or
was his face more like Botswana, an ever-shrinking
idea made to look like real land in the shade of the
planes wing, didn't Jim appear far from you and
your touch, like Sudan, Libya, Senegal, Egypt?
Wasn't
he already a lost cause, a country of a friend whose
name you can't recall unless sufficiently drunk on
holiday? You left a broken man, returned a foolish
hero. Hollywood reporter said come see the
funniest man in the world. Variety said funny man
swears to no longer use the word nigger, but we
knew the truth. One of us went home, came back
with more niggas than he left with.

For the Easter Yellow Marshmallow Peep, Smashed on the Department Store Floor

Wednesday will always
be jealous of Tuesday,
no matter the season.

Everyone wants closer
to Sunday. We all wish
for holy, each of us
comes up short.

Jesus and Mary Magdalene- The Last Night Together, the Final Miracle

He removes his shoes
before entering her
bedchamber, knows
this is holy ground

She left blood over
door entrance to
keep the holy spirit
in the room, not out

Mattress made of henna,
pillows stitched of their
ancestors hair, no clothes
touch this bed

The first time they made
love, the next morning-
fish, fruit, gold pieces,
cured lamb—were in the
foyer of the hut—gifts
from those grateful for
being within earshot

Tonight,
he has saved a miracle
just for her. As they make
love, join and fuse in a
myriad of sinew, bone,

rib, teeth bared, some-times in a
smile, hips melted wax on a wall
forgotten—he pulls the sweat
from their skin, makes it round,
spherical, perfect in its wetness,
pulls it from between them gives
it an orbit just over their bed, till
heat threatens to make them
slaves, forcing him to call upon
his makeshift raincloud

He never notices; her face,
before the storm was already
wet, her eyes saying what the
mouth was forbidden-In the
morning you must go to
Damascus, never to return.

Why They Call Me Tina

I have legs on loan from Artemis Rumor
is, my daddy was part centaur/ part wood
sprite
My mother was a cocktease goddess,
running naked with her virgins hunting
in his woods

He dared to catch her, ensnare her in
his net
Kissed without warning nor permission her
sunburned skin
Unable to outrun her, unable to
withstand another arrow, he turned
himself into a tree

Artemis cut off his engorged branch,
made a flute from it

Had I known my lineage I never would
have been your groupie, Ike
Legs built from deep south gin mills,
illegal juke joint hooch machines, bone
spurs fashioned out of crushed mason
jars
I was Gullah and Goddess and didn't know it

Didn't know I had Cadillacs for knees, oil in
place of sap pumping thru arteries, didn't
know my ass ran on diesel

But at the core of it all,

I am borne of wood

Artemis would spend her non-hunting days
playing her flute, often off-key and much to her
own amusement, not caring

With every note, a nymph would freeze to death,
a minotaur seize up, become infertile, a wood sprite chew
its' own wrists, crying as the sap ran free
All over the world, protectors of the forest would
petrify themselves to stop the incessant longing, the
fevered passion so strong in them to own her and that
sound

Ike, I forgive you every black eye Given
the choice, every man wants to destroy a
God they cannot control
I imagine how hard it must have been for
you some nights-
on stage with your girl, your song,
your band, your show, my music

My music
Not the guttural growl from my lips, but
those legs, smooth, thick, unforgiving,
fusing with cheap pumps and pumping,
some viscious gyration, everywhere at
once a great pistoning, movement into
movement

Nothing funky about those thighs, Ike

Nothing jazzy, no monotone, no 3/4
timing, no Sarah Vaughn, no Shirelles, no
Gladys Knight. Just a little Janis Joplin
mixed with Patti LaBelle drunk and
making babies at 5 a.m.
Babies made of wood and blood
attached to the waist of a simple
southern girl with an ugly name

Legs stronger than the ones Jesus used to walk
on water, my daddy was wood and my mama
was mean and here we are
in this emergency room, this bedroom, this
backstage Ed Sullivan, this green room Dick Clark,
this London trip, this chitlin circuit outhouse, this
home studio, this bullshit biopic, this several kids
later, this Buddhist temple, this place where the
incense burns clear, this shitty little hotel room–

twenty dollars to my name but priceless legs,
looking at the years on my face and the bruises on
my heart, and I can't muster the energy to get
pissed, get mad, get even

All I can do is let my hands sweep past radio dials till
music erupts, and let the best part of me take over

All I can do is stand up, and dance
(on your grave)
dance

(for your salvation)
dance
(for my mama)
dance

My mother was Artemis
and was one bad bitch
My father was part wood
sprite, part centaur-
a hopeless romantic

I was named Tina
so you could own me
I was named Anna Mae
so you could find me

But they call me Tina now because
Jesus was already taken, and our
God,
He be a jealous God

"If one is lucky enough to come across mr mabrey's work, you may find yourself luckier still, to find the experience of having a poet possessed by some of the shake of them great holy ghosts that sometimes shake us all, and for that poet possessed to move your body like he was possessing yours--like a spirit haunting a house, curling himself around your spine and not letting go until both of you are too tired to move, and like an exorcism in reverse, you may walk out that house haunting a little shook, a little scared and a little more appreciative of the skin you still wear. There is intensity in this man, and an intense splendor to be had from the work he shares."

Anis Mojgani
Two time Individual National Poetry Slam Champion

Blue Baby

Hey you
Been watching you
with your heartburn
and half moons

You been smiling too much
and laughing obscenely loud
laughs too little

Who told you to smirk?
What prick forbade you
from picking adult swim
laughs, cartoon chuckles

Be deliciously evil
Mondark's laugh holds
more melody

Sprinkle bullets in your cereal
Shit Greyhound buses all over this
land. Your cock is a tour bus
Where ya goin tonight?
Somewhere pretty, exotic?

Drive balls to the wall
Your balls are Gregorian
Chants- Ohm!
Latinize that shit
Snort feathers and sneeze
birds, flocks of birds

Your nose is a penguin and your eyes
disco balls Everybody dance the
penguin glitter dance. Don't you hush
hush

Speak that bubblespit sermon
Kiss like you got peanut butter
stuck to the roof of your mouth

Your mouth is a rain dance
Your mouth is a home
for broken fences
Your mouth is a gazebo
Your mouth is a fenceless
yard

Your mouth is not moving
Your lips are blue
Your mouth is so pretty
that it's purdy

Use your mouth
There's a stallion
on your tongue
Giddy yap horsey
Giddyap

You got canyons to plunder
You don't ride the dark whale
for nine months of solitary
To die in a bassinet. They don't
make tombstones that small

You got breasts to suckle
You got warm milk on the stove You
come out that fleshy oven black, white,
yellow, olive, not blue

Anything but blue

You get up now
You breathe
You got all of Saturday morning
Waiting for you
Mr. Cereal, Mrs. Milk
Cousin Cartoon

You got plenty of time for
the blues
Blue-lipped, blue skin
Blue baby baby baby
You're scaring Sunday sermon
You get up little choo choo

This here's a nursery
a dance floor, the O.K. Corral not a
grave Laugh now, please

Rejection Letter

(after not getting into Cave Canem- an exercise in venting)

Maybe it was your cologne, too
much finesse, not enough Hai
Karate, or your words, laced
with E Pluribus Unum but no money, no old
money, no blue blood Kentucky grass
smellin' money. No Witchita in yo Kansas,
no Tar in your Heel. Heavy on your Brand
News but light in your Jamiroquai.

P'rhaps iT Was Ur Sy(i)ntax.

Or your lazy overabundance. How much
Teddy Pendergrass is enough, how much
Curtis Mayfield- too much? Nigg-a or Nigg-
uh, said with a whoosh, a impenetrable sigh,
lush wonderment in your tooth whistle, a
sound only uttered when naked, sweating,
and layered in sheets of sin, fan overhead
panting like a many tongued rabid dog,
amazed at what it just witnessed... that
sound.

Perhaps your inbetween between lines weren't
shattered enough, splintered and fractured, like
a kerrigan femur, broken but not cracked right,
like raising arizona back from the dead a day
too late,

to find stench behind the cloak, blood
on the dagger, and lucille clifton's clit
high in the horizon, like a sun, like a moon,
like a plump star beckoning you to follow it
with no particular place to go, a wild look
in its' eyes, like Chuck Berry catching a
reflection of himself in two-way dressing
room mirror, watching, watching little girls,
little teenage girls strip, strip, unsheathe
layers of legs while he humps bumps and
strokes to a sweaty degree on the other
side, sees himself, those eyes, ravenous
old wolves too long in the forest, have
taken to eating their own leg.

Eureka! You didn't introduce your Pablo. Pablo
the innocent, Pablo the brave, Pablo with red
nipples over Spain's belly, Chilean testicles,
heavyweighted balls lost at sea, Pablo the
resourceful, tearing a flag to shreds, planting
pieces in the ground, calling for Matilde to come
and shit his till, fertilize a revolution.

No Octavio, I say, I got this one. No
Ernesto, your assistance is not required. No
Davies, No Smith, No Yusef, No Sally, No
Nikki, Stay back e.e., Move to the rear of
the room DuBois, Marjorie, Thompson,
Shut your mouth Ellis, This seat's taken
Walt, same goes for you Karl, bastards,

to the last one of you I say- Ha! and Ha! See?
See the loss in the pierced heart? What hymn
made of sangria do you plead, or fifth of Jack,
Glenlivet, Single Malted liar, Irish hope,
Tuscany grape, save your tears, I am not thirsty
for anything man made.

Bring me God's heart so that I might chew it
lazily, with no sudden tearing or ripping noises,
just a casual meal between us friends. Oh, great
depression, now you wish to go on vacation, on
leave, sun yourself on some foreigner's shore
with arms around you that are not mine?
Take the doors from my house, and the mirrors, let my
reflection be on the passing traffic, those breezes
created by steel and cold, honest winds all of them,
made by the motion of going somewhere, getting
somewhere.

Where will I go now? There is a plane on its strip full of short
skirted women and alcohol, businessmen with propositions
and lies to tell, obnoxious families with Norman Rockwell for
a backdrop, manufactured children who know the pitch to
sing and scream, to disturb my drugged sleep, restrooms to
cramped and judgmental to grant me space to masturbate,
fanfare, magazines, Nyquil-laced amaretto, eye masks, neck
pillows, window seat, headphones, Sonny Rollins on a
tortured repeat, shoes off, deep, cleansing breaths, in the
nose- out the mouth, sleep on the tip of my tongue, and my
eyes, and my ears, and my toes, and my fingers.

On the wing, a rejection letter sits, stares in at me. Makes the plane cant just a little to the left, makes the world five minutes late for every important thing, Sits like a seatbelt drawn too tight. I can't breathe.

Loving Constantine
(for LaToya)

First—Practice saying her name.
Begin with one hundred times a day.
Work up to five hundred. Rest on
Sundays. Take pictures of your smile,
chart improved whiteness, compare to
before you knew her.

Second—Take every letter in her name from
the bible. Just scratch them out. Reread entire
thing. Observe how less holy it now feels.

Third—Make a car, a jet, a couch, a chair, a
fountain pen, and a set of knives based solely on
the inspiration in her hips.

Fourth—Always go to bed last. Bottle her
exhalations while she sleeps. Freeze them for
mixed drinks and sun tea.
Keep them in your water bottle when you
hit the gym.

Fifth—Check her shoulder blades for
knobby areas, and protrusions, anything
that might reveal traces of where her
wings once were. take one feather from
her pillow, burn it, check her sleeping
face for discomfort. See if she twitches.

Longina

With a rose between your teeth, your
hair pulled back high, like an eclipse
against your face, with seafoam
underfoot, soaking the carpet,
staining your skirt's hem with salts,
both old and strong in taste and
smell, come to me.

With eyes untouched
by time and the lips of liars, eyes
full of brown, of chocolate, of cocoa,
thick liquid, powder mixed with the
spices of your teary gaze, a heady
brew reserved for monarchs celebrating
cinco de mayo, eyes that have seen
virgins sacrificed on the altar, their blood
not red, but bark, red bricks flowing
from their slight necks, sacrificed for
the harvest, for the drought, for the
famine, for rain, for heat, for cold,
for food, for the festival, for the secrets, oh,
all those little kingdom destroying secrets
your eyes have witnessed, how deep those
eddies and streams must run in you, those
eyes, with those eyes, see me.

With hands, fingers made by the gods of the
piano, viola, and violin, of all things weight
sensitive and pressurized, all things made of
catgut and high strung

awaiting one who knows how to make them speak,
someone like you, fingers like yours, protected
from the blacksmith's fire yet unafraid of the
hearth and heat, the grain bowl, comfortable
around the neck of a fowl, snapping it so smooth
you would think it asleep rather than dead, but
dead you pluck, nimble hands hold the knife, make
it whisper secrets in the skin, let the blood, drain
the waste, portion and cook, make music from the
slaughter, a concerto from the carnage, those
hands, with those hands-touch me.

Staccato

Around midnight
above skyline
at adam's apple-
kiss me

Between raindrops
before yesterday
because of Mandela-
kiss me

Caught in amber
close to sunrise
chasing Chicago-
kiss me

Dawn approaching
damn the hour
drive your purpose-
kiss me

Exorcise vices
entice my swelling
excite all tomorrows-
kiss me

Free freedom
feed my forest
frost every windshield-
kiss me

Grab time
give thanks for lips
gyrate the hourglass-
kiss me

Hold precious
hand me heaven in pieces
heat up every Paris-
kiss me

Straight Edged Razor and the Lustful Wrist

There's a shine to it, elegant, a last
dance of sorts runs from hilt to tip.
Hold it in your hand, turn it over,
fondle pearl lips, feel stainless
tongue flicker a light nudge, a coax
to kiss deeper, open her up, flirt her
into talk-ing to you, telling you all
the things she's seen, all the sights
she can show.

Press thumb against her throat,
notice how easy the tongue laps at
your palm, slithers between middle
and third finger.

Close your eyes, listen for the lust in
your blood as it rises, hear veins throb
against the crotch of skin.
Pulse is a tone seductive, melancholy
muses only for the hearty, lean back your
arm till it is all wrist, all bent, all time,
all those precious whispers in the nook
of your palm, stories of crimson and
lilac, thunder and the forever no- no's:
small of a woman's back, the pressing
desire to swipe at a misplaced strand of
hair on a perfect stranger, the hunger for
raw meat, blood pooling in the corner

of a mouth, a broken nose, ripe as a
broken heart and just as romantic.

Hear her incantations, look at your own wrist,
follow the crescent mouth inside, watch it
bubble to the surface, begin to speak back to
her mystic, this, this is the language you
thought was land familiar, thought was home,
but no, your hearth has a flame older than this
moment, older than purple, back to when blue
was only blue was only blue and black sat high
on a throne and grew fat on the bones of lesser
thoughts. This is not your fight to lose, nor
yours to win, just a body, just a map you are,
another contour, another angle, too bulbous
and slack filled to be a threat, best you silence
your steps and let these two, old friends, foes,
and siblings, have their petty conversation.

If they choose to talk, to argue, to…kiss, relax
knowing all conversation between steel and flesh
ends in a stalemate, never settled in the slice, in
the quick blur, the movement, gushing flow, such
a deep kiss, this straight edged fellatio is a
schoolgirl crush between goddesses equinox old
and too tired to find a new form of
communication.

Weeds and Roy Ayers

Tulips in the vase
Roses in the trash
Dandelions in the yard
My snooze button
has a black eye
The bloody teeth
in its' mouth read
12:00
p.m or a.m
it doesn't matter
I watch it flash
with eyes analog red
and lids to heavy
for a wednesday

The church sent me tulips
a woman with a soft voice
and no doubt fat ankles
called to see if I needed
anything
Had to bite my tongue
to stop from saying the
obvious

Could I have my husband back

A man
think his name is ted
though to me
he's always looked
like

a bill
maybe a frank
brought me roses
said he felt he'd waited
the appropriate amount
of time before approaching
maybe a movie
or dinner
there's a great little place
not far from work
that's quiet
(too quiet)
intimate
(too small)
has a nice booth
in the back
(too small too dark)
we could just talk
or I could talk
and he could just
listen

But what's there to say
billfrankted you don't really
want the truth anymore than the
church wants to know if there
is anything they can do for me

Because the truth is
the only flowers
that matter anymore

are the dandelions
growing in the yard
outside and who's going to
cut those little sunbathers
who's going to get on
their hands and knees
and pull them out
one by one
at the root
who's going to chase me
around the yard
or the pool
or catch me getting
dressed for church
putting earrings in for work
getting undressed in the kitchen
catch me naked in the laundry room
and pin me down
like the little girl I used to be and
rub those yellow talisman on my
cheeks
till there's sunshine
on my face

Who's going to fertilize my garden
Who's going to drink my lemonade
Who's going to put
sunshine
on my face
now

Robert Johnson: Live at the Dockery Plantation
(how Sekou Sundiata learned to play the blues)

For Sekou Sundiata and Umar Bin Hasan

Push that music boy
Get the mandolin out your throat
Make room for the
Congo and beat pan
tambourine and cymbal
Smack the steel sunshine
caress the brass discus
Can you make it sing
make it blow
make it hurt
hurt us

One for the downbeat
two for the ladies line
One for the upswing
two for the plucked bass

The bass
The baseman cometh
with no regard for your politic
Arms built from leftover iron and
forgotten train tracks Watch'em
run up that vein Run vein run
Man got a jukebox in each fingertip
calluses got mouths
singing in the key of blood

Bleed now Joe
Call'em Joe they say
Say what you will
Say old man in corner
Bag of bones and a sack of skin in
a seersucker suit
Soothsayer in seersucker sees
things differently-
Look close now

See the holes in the index and thumb
too many late night battles
too much time on gladiator bandstands
Stages made of gin and other unnamed hooch
mason jars, shuck n jive, shoeshine polish pickled
pigs feet on corner bar
Jar half off like a dare
like a challenge
like her legs at the third table
No, from *your* left Never mind

Look at those holes Look through
his fingers and see old Satan
smiling on the other side Devil
can play a mean 6 string But not
like Joe
Mighty Joe

New school fill up finger holes with superglue
Smack the counter
Take a shot
Get back on the battlefield
Not Joe

He fills finger hole pain
with molasses he keep in his guitar case
Makes the music sweet
makes the blues put on lipstick
'fore she bite your jugular

Slave pick the cotton
Nigga pick the strings
Slave pick the cotton
Nigga pick the strings

Slave Nigga Baseman
Baseman Slave Negro
Baseman a slave to the string
like Negro a slave to being a slave
Shake his hand I dare you
Don't do it
It's a trap
See, see, see?
How he shake?
Soft, palm first
Fingers last
Like a patch of jasmine
or something pretty and purple
in some field you ain't invited to
There's the trick never meeting your eye

shoulder stooped
hat tipped low to hide his ignorance...?
No-
To hide his *eyes*
(what used to be)
Lost his originals in a crap shoot
(kept on playing though) much to
the Devil's chagrin

The hat hides the fire
hides the revelation
hides the frogs
the bees
the dust storm
the fucking-
the pure fucking of it all

All day/all night those eyes used to fuck
in God's name
He'd fuck
over under besides in spite of
rain or snow or whirlwind
or church or God's mighty presence
even in the crossroads

Shake his hand if you want
I did it once
Couldn't sleep for 6 days
couldn't eat for two
couldn't see to my wives needs for...well
never you mind that But know this-

She came to him
Just as sure if he'd called her

Gentlemen callers picking toes
behind the curtain of chance
Ladies of the evening fanning
bosoms, spreading their legs
He on the stage weapon in hand
Me too dumb and deaf mute to holla
(not much good it would've done)
He so much as plucked one chord-there
she go

Skirt in her hands like a flag of surrender
Her scent tripping over its own feet to get in his nose
She dancing up front like some French whore
some can can
some can-can
and some will-will
and others do-do the do

Ten cents for a dance your soul for a song
Ten cents for a dance your soul for a song

Sing song sing song
Lord knows I tried
I ran home/put on my Sunday best took
another bath cleaned the house
jumped the broom and threw salt
over my left shoulder

boiled greens
swore I'd study war no more
But when I came back it was
too late
He'd started that fatal song/
She, her final dance Archangel
Michael and old Llegba
arm in arm hooting and hollering
coaxing her on
And Joe

Joe makes sounds like his fingers are
schoolgirls passing notes from the
strings to his mouth

Then he turned them eyes on me
Blacker than a coal miner's heart
darker than my daddies hands like he
done swallowed every
bad thing in the world like he know what it
means to get your ass whupped by heaven
and hell, get up, dust yourself off, and ask
for seconds

I ain't ashamed to say I lost control of my bowels my
functions my up my down my can kicking ran off into
the night
Didn't stop till I heard something snap inside me
thought it was my bone
turned out it was something
deeper than that

passed out
Didn't know who or what I was till you turned me on my back
Now imagine my surprise when you ask me how to get there
how to meet the man
(if you can call him a man any more than you can call me
alive)
I warn you to go back where you came but
I know you won't listen neither did I

So here's what you do—
Go to the crossroads
any crossroads boy don't matter which just
make sure it's made of dirt or keep some in
your pocket
and he'll come
call him by name
He got so many you can't go wrong Just
stand at the crossroads with your guitar
case open and one dollar in it take all
your strings out, then call him

Call him Los Angeles
Detroit
Dayton
and New Orleans
Call him Capetown and Soweto
Call him Babel and Brooklyn
Call him Alabama and Little Rock
Call him Magnolia and hallelujah Jesus

Call him Wormwood or Paul
Call him Caesar and Mohammed
Call him X call him warrior
Call him Loki call him the great trickster
Call him Jimi call him Ruth
Call him King Solomon Mines
Call him kimosabe Call him
Osama
Call him George
Call him Tricky Dick
Call him heroin
Call him mint julep tea
Call him indentured servitude
Call him carpet bag
Call him Satchmo
Call him Janis
Call him Mau Mau and Navajo
Call him slaughterhouse and shotgun
Call him the whole book of Psalms
or Jude
or death
or rainmaker
or the screamer
or Nina
Call him the rock
Call him Philadelphia
Call him emancipation
and the king of broken dreams
Call him fools gold
or gallows or tired rope
Call him spoiled gin
Call him hound's-tooth
Call him buffalo soldier

Then when you hear the sweetest music your
ears ever tried to stand
A voice your mind can't quite wrap around
you'll see him walking a piece aways holes in
his fingers which do not bleed hands soft as
purple wrapped round a neck of a guitar
dragging against the dirt road kicking up sparks
that sound like every train you missed
coming back to get you Then you'll blink
and he'll be standing right there in front of you like
he was there all along waiting for you

His hat will be tipped low
His dirty suit smells of jasmine and clove His
rotted teeth with breath like your lovers and
you'll hear him say *My name is Joe/ Heard you
wanted to learn how to play the blues* Only cost
you a dollar at first

But if you want to be the best
then you gotta challenge him
play him for your soul you'll
remember is shaking his hand

Praise God and shame the devil
Praise God and shame the devil
Dance with the devil better learn your steps
But you can't beat the Devil with no
Soft shoe shuck n' jive
He got jukeboxes in his fingers with the sounds of slain souls
He got jukeboxes in his fingers filled with the sounds of slain souls

www.ingramcontent.com/pod-product-compliance
Lightning Source LLC
Chambersburg PA
CBHW060656100426
42734CB00047B/1950